WITHDRAW
from records of
Mid-Continent Public Library

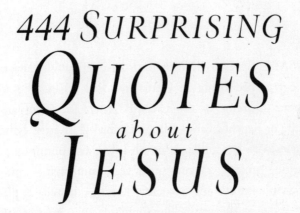

444 SURPRISING
QUOTES
about
JESUS

A Treasury of Inspiring Thoughts & Classic Quotations

232 F825   APR   2006

444 surprising quotes about
  Jesus

I0640030

Dr. ISABELLA D. BUNN is both an international lawyer and a theologian specializing in Christian social ethics. She serves as Associate Director of the Oxford Center for Christianity and Culture at Regent's Park College, Oxford University. Isabella collaborates with her husband, novelist T. Davis Bunn, on a variety of writing projects. Having spent years rummaging around antiquarian bookstores and academic libraries, Isabella is pleased to share some of the compelling thoughts that have captured her mind and imagination.

444 SURPRISING
QUOTES
about
JESUS

A Treasury of Inspiring Thoughts & Classic Quotations

COMPILED BY

Isabella D. Bunn

BETHANY HOUSE PUBLISHERS

Minneapolis, Minnesota

MID-CONTINENT PUBLIC LIBRARY
North Oak Branch
8700 N. Oak Trafficway
Kansas City, MO 64155

NO

MID-CONTINENT PUBLIC LIBRARY

3 0000 12714435 4

444 Surprising Quotes About Jesus
Copyright © 2006
Isabella D. Bunn

Cover design by Kevin Keller

Unless otherwise identified, Scripture quotations are from the HOLY BIBLE, NEW INTERNATIONAL VERSION®. Copyright © 1973, 1978, 1984 by International Bible Society. Used by permission of Zondervan Publishing House. All rights reserved.

Scripture quotations identified KJV are from the King James Version of the Bible.

Scripture quotations identified NLT are from the *Holy Bible*, New Living Translation, copyright © 1996. Used by permission of Tyndale House Publishers, Inc., Wheaton, Illinois 60189. All rights reserved.

All rights reserved. No part of this publication may be reproduced, stored in a retrieval system, or transmitted in any form or by any means—electronic, mechanical, photocopying, recording, or otherwise—without the prior written permission of the publisher and copyright owners.

Published by Bethany House Publishers
11400 Hampshire Avenue South
Bloomington, Minnesota 55438

Bethany House Publishers is a division of
Baker Publishing Group, Grand Rapids, Michigan.

Printed in the United States of America

Library of Congress Cataloging-in-Publication Data

444 surprising quotes about Jesus : a treasury of inspiring thoughts and classic quotations / compiled by Isabella D. Bunn.
 p. cm.
 Summary: "Drawn from sources ancient and modern, this thought-provoking and inspirational collection of quotes cites everyone from famous political leaders to humble pastors. Who is Jesus? Long-time Christians as well as spiritual seekers will discover some answers in this book. A perfect library addition for pastors, students, and quote collectors"—Provided by publisher.
 Includes bibliographical references and index.
 ISBN 0-7642-0161-1 (pbk.)
 1. Jesus Christ—Quotations. I. Title: Four hundred and forty-four surprising quotes about Jesus. II. Bunn, Isabella.
 BT199.A14   2006
 232—dc22   2005032507

Contents

PREFACE

To think about what has been thought about Jesus is a revelation in itself.

As I leafed through hundreds of volumes spanning the centuries, I encountered both the God and the Man of religion, history, philosophy, art. Some responses to Jesus are grounded in the intellect; surely no one has been subject to more intense study and exposition. Other expressions are inspired by faith—prayer and praise and worship. Many reflections center on relationships—Christ as savior, shepherd, king, and Son of God. A range of ideas links Jesus to doctrinal questions of incarnation, salvation, resurrection. Some enter into the life of Christ with passion and imagination, distilling the moments of his existence that have become turning points in ours. Still others unveil how his human example and divine power continue to transform lives and circumstances.

Working to gather a collection of such thoughts has engaged my mind and heart and soul, sometimes in surprising ways. I experienced a sense of intimacy and awe, of clarity and mystery, of finitude and timelessness. As I came to know more of him, I was humbled by how little I knew.

For over two millennia, Jesus of Nazareth has provoked an astonishing range of reactions. My hope is that this book encourages us to consider anew the question Jesus asked of his own disciples: "Who do you say that I am?"

JESUS AS GOD AND MAN

As soon as Jesus was baptized, he went up out of the water. At that moment heaven was opened, and he saw the Spirit of God descending like a dove and lighting on him. And a voice from heaven said, "This is my Son, whom I love; with him I am well pleased."

MATTHEW 3:16–17

Jesus Christ, the condescension of divinity, and the exaltation of humanity.

PHILLIPS BROOKS (1835–1893)
BISHOP OF MASSACHUSETTS

To be a Christian is to believe in the impossible. Jesus was God. Jesus was Human.

MADELEINE L'ENGLE
AMERICAN AWARD-WINNING WRITER

[Jesus] is a divine figure sent down from the celestial world of light, the Son of the Most High coming forth from the Father, veiled in earthly form and inaugurating the redemption through his work.

RUDOLPH BULTMANN (1884-1976)
GERMAN THEOLOGIAN

Following the Holy Fathers, we all with one voice confess our Lord Jesus Christ to be one and the same Son, perfect in divinity and humanity, truly God and truly human, consisting of a rational soul and a body, being of one substance with the Father in relation to His divinity, and being of one substance with us in relation to His humanity. . . .

THE COUNCIL OF CHALCEDON, 451

The Son whose birth from the Father is unsearchable was born in another birth which can be searched out. By the one birth we should learn that his greatness has no limits, by the other we may recognize that his grace has no measure.

EPHRAEM THE SYRIAN (C. 303-373)
CHURCH FATHER AND WRITER OF COMMENTARIES
"HOMILY ON OUR LORD"

The Divine Vision still was seen,
Still was the Human Form Divine,
Weeping in weak & mortal clay,
O Jesus, still the Form was thine.

And thine the Human Face, & thine
The Human Hands & Feet & Breath,
Entering thro' the Gates of Birth
And passing thro' the Gates of Death.

WILLIAM BLAKE (1757–1827)
BRITISH POET, ARTIST AND MYSTIC
"JERUSALEM"

Jesus Christ in an incomprehensible way veiled the
divine nature with finite human nature, and from the
finite human nature he displayed the actions
of the infinite God.

IGNATII BRIANCHANINOV (1807–1867)
RUSSIAN BISHOP

Christ, therefore, is one, perfect God and perfect
Man; and Him we worship along with the Father and
the Spirit. . . . We worship Him not as mere flesh,
but as flesh united with Divinity, and because His
two natures are brought under the one Person and
one subsistence of God the Word.

ST. JOHN OF DAMASCUS (C. 675-749)
GREEK THEOLOGIAN
"EXPOSITIONS OF THE ORTHODOX FAITH"

We call Mary's child "Emmanuel" because we see
in him the God who has always been with us, always
in the midst. There is no need for him to intervene
as a stranger from the outside world.
He is already here.

JOHN V. TAYLOR
ANGLICAN BISHOP OF WINCHESTER
THE GO-BETWEEN GOD, 1972

At the name of Jesus every knee shall bow,
Every tongue confess him King of Glory now;
'Tis the Father's pleasure we should call him Lord,
Who from the beginning was the mighty Word.

CAROLINE MARIA NOEL (1817-1877)
ENGLISH HYMN WRITER
HYMN, "THE NAME OF JESUS," 1870

The properties of each nature and substance were preserved in their totality, and came together to form one person. Humility was assumed by majesty, weakness by strength, mortality by eternity; and to pay the debt that we had incurred, an inviolable nature was united to a nature that can suffer.

POPE LEO I (FIFTH CENTURY)
"ST. LEO THE GREAT," BORN IN TUSCANY
LETTER, 449

In his moral sonship to God Jesus Christ is not a median figure, half God, half man; he is a single person wholly directed as man toward God and wholly directed in his unity with the father toward men.

H. RICHARD NIEBUHR (1894-1962)
PROFESSOR OF CHRISTIAN ETHICS AT YALE DIVINITY SCHOOL
CHRIST AND CULTURE, 1951

Every passage in the history of our Lord and Savior is of unfathomable depth, and affords inexhaustible matter of contemplation. All that concerns Him is infinite, and what we first discern is but the surface of that which begins and ends in eternity.

JOHN HENRY NEWMAN (1801-1890)
ENGLISH CARDINAL AND LEADER OF THE OXFORD MOVEMENT
"DISCOURSES TO MIXED CONGREGATIONS"

For the Christian believer and theologian, the Agony in the Garden is one of the most solemn moments in the Passion. It is the point where Christ in his human nature wishes that the cup of suffering could pass from him, but in his divine nature he knows that he, and he alone, can take upon himself the expiatory death which will deliver the world from sin.

A. N. WILSON
ENGLISH JOURNALIST AND BIOGRAPHER
JESUS: A LIFE, 1992

What does the Church think of Christ? The Church's answer is categorical and uncompromising, and it is this: That Jesus Bar-Joseph, the carpenter of Nazareth, was in fact and in truth, and in the most exact and literal sense of the words, the God "by whom all things were made." . . . He was in every respect a genuine living man. He was not merely a man so good as to be "like God"—He was God.

DOROTHY L. SAYERS (1893-1957)
ENGLISH NOVELIST AND CHRISTIAN APOLOGIST

If ever man was God or God man, Jesus Christ was both.

LORD BYRON (1788-1824)
ENGLISH POET

He fulfilled all things by the humanity that he had taken, for those who only in that way were able to appreciate his divinity.

EUSEBIUS OF CAESAREA (C. 260-341)
THEOLOGIAN AND "FATHER OF CHURCH HISTORY"
"THE DEMONSTRATION OF THE GOSPEL"

He does not cease to be God because He becomes Man, nor fail to be Man because He remains forever God. This is the true faith for human blessedness, to preach at once the Godhead and the manhood, to confess the Word and the flesh, neither forgetting the God, because He is man, nor ignoring the flesh, because He is the Word.

HILARY OF POITIERS (FOURTH CENTURY)
BISHOP OF POITIERS AND THEOLOGIAN
"ON THE TRINITY"

The really staggering Christian claim is that Jesus of Nazareth was God made man. . . .
The more you think about it, the more staggering it gets. Nothing in fiction is so fantastic as is this truth of the Incarnation.

JAMES I. PACKER
BRITISH EVANGELICAL THEOLOGIAN AND WRITER
KNOWING GOD, 1993

Remember, Christ was not a deified man, neither was he a humanized God. He was perfectly God and at the same time perfectly man.

CHARLES HADDON SPURGEON (1834–1892)
ENGLISH NONCONFORMIST PREACHER

In Jesus Christ heaven meets earth and earth ascends to heaven.

HENRY LAW (1797–1884)
ENGLISH ANGLICAN EVANGELICAL WRITER

Once faced with the staggering proposition that He is God, I was cornered, all avenues of retreat blocked, no falling back to that comfortable middle ground about Jesus being a great moral teacher. For what He taught includes the assertion that He is indeed God. And if He is not, that one statement alone would have to qualify as the most monstrous lie of all time—stripping Him at once of any possible moral platform.

CHARLES COLSON
FORMER WHITE HOUSE COUNSEL
AND FOUNDER OF PRISON FELLOWSHIP
BORN AGAIN, 1972
(ACCOUNT OF HIS CONVERSION,
DURING THE WATERGATE INVESTIGATION)

He is mediator because He is both God and man. He holds within Himself the entire intimate world of divinity, the entire Mystery of the Trinity, and the mystery both of temporal life and of immortality. He is true man. In Him the divine is not confused with the human. There remains something essentially divine. But at the same time Christ is so human! Thanks to this, the entire world of men, the entire history of humanity, finds in Him its expression before God.

POPE JOHN PAUL II (1920–2005)
POLISH PRIEST AND PHILOSOPHER
CROSSING THE THRESHOLD OF HOPE, 1994

If God never became flesh, like us, he could neither redeem us nor reveal to us his promise of eternal life. It is only by becoming like us that God can make us like him, restoring us in his image.

ST. IRENAEUS (C. 130–202)
BISHOP OF LYONS

By the Incarnation, God became man; that is to say, the two natures, divine and human, are found united in the person of Christ. What is less well known to those who adhere to this mystery by faith is the astonishing transformation which He introduced into all nature and consequently into the manner in which we must henceforth conceive it. One ought rather to say the astonishing transformations, for this mystery includes in it so many others that one would never have done considering the consequences of it.

ÉTIENNE HENRY GILSON (1884–1978)
FRENCH PROFESSOR OF MEDIEVAL PHILOSOPHY
CHRISTIANITY AND PHILOSOPHY, 1939

God only wants one thing from us: that we live according to his laws. And he has shown us how to do this by putting his Son on earth in human form. Thus by imitating the example of Christ we offer to God all the worship he requires.

JUSTIN MARTYR (c. 100–165)
CHRISTIAN APOLOGIST, BORN IN PALESTINIAN SYRIA

I am trying here to prevent anyone saying the really foolish thing that people often say about Him: "I'm ready to accept Jesus as a great moral teacher, but I don't accept His claim to be God." That is the one thing we must not say. A man who was merely a man and said the sort of things Jesus said would not be a great moral teacher. He would either be a lunatic—on a level with the man who says he is a poached egg—or else he would be the Devil of Hell. You must make

your choice. Either this man was, and is, the Son of God: or else a madman or something worse. You can shut Him up for a fool, you can spit at Him and kill Him as a demon; or you can fall at His feet and call Him Lord and God. But let us not come with any patronising nonsense about His being a great human teacher. He has not left that open to us.
He did not intend to.

C. S. LEWIS (CLIVE STAPLES LEWIS) (1898–1963)
IRISH LITERARY SCHOLAR,
CHRISTIAN APOLOGIST AND WRITER
MERE CHRISTIANITY, 1943

O Lord Jesus Christ, make me worthy to understand the profound mystery of your holy incarnation, which you have worked for our sake and for our salvation. Truly there is nothing so great and wonderful as this, that you, my God, who are the creator of all things, should become a creature, so that we should become like God. You have humbled yourself and made yourself small that we might be made mighty. You have taken the form of a servant, so that you might confer upon us a royal and divine beauty.

ANGELA OF FOLGINO (1248–1309)
ITALIAN MYSTIC

The power and attraction Jesus Christ exercises over men never comes from him alone, but from him as Son of the Father. . . . Even when theologies fail to do justice to this fact, Christians living with Christ in their cultures are aware of it. For they are forever being challenged to abandon all things for the sake of God; and forever being sent back into the world to teach and practice all the things that have been commanded them.

H. RICHARD NIEBUHR (1894–1962)
PROFESSOR OF CHRISTIAN ETHICS AT YALE DIVINITY SCHOOL
CHRIST AND CULTURE, 1951

The death of Socrates, philosophizing quietly with his friends, is the pleasantest that one could desire: that of Jesus, expiring amid torments, insulted, railed at, cursed by a whole nation, is the most horrible that anyone could fear. Socrates, taking the poisoned cup, blesses him who presents it, and who weeps beside him. Jesus, in the midst of frightful anguish, prays for his maddened executioners. Yes! If the life and death of Socrates are those of a philosopher, the life and death of Jesus are those of a God.

JEAN-JACQUES ROUSSEAU (1712–1778)
SWISS-FRENCH PHILOSOPHER AND NOVELIST
ÉMILE, 1762

Thou art the King of Glory O Christ.
Thou are the everlasting Son of the Father.

THE BOOK OF COMMON PRAYER, 1662
"TE DEUM"

God has revealed Himself to us through Jesus Christ,
and Jesus is revealed to us through the Bible.
Therefore, one of the greatest treasures to be derived
from Bible-reading is knowing God through focusing
on the attributes of Christ—attributes that then
become a rich source for our praise.

ANNE GRAHAM LOTZ
BIBLE TEACHER AND FOUNDER OF ANGEL MINISTRIES
THE VISION OF HIS GLORY, 1996

As the only person to come from eternity to earth,
then return to eternity, Jesus knows the whole truth—
past, present and future—and can give you a
one-of-a-kind perspective.

BRUCE WILKERSON
FOUNDER OF WALK THRU THE BIBLE MINISTRIES
A LIFE GOD REWARDS, 2002

A virgin birth seems a most appropriate and creative
way for God to enter His world.

PAUL SMITH
QUOTED IN *HIS MIRACLES*, 2004

One who is looking for proofs that God manifested himself to us in the flesh must look to his activities. . . . The wonders evident in his actions we regard as sufficient proof of the presence of the Godhead, and in the deeds recorded we mark all those attributes by which the divine nature is characterized.

ST. GREGORY OF NYSSA (C. 335-394)
CAPPODOCIAN CHURCH FATHER
"ADDRESS ON RELIGIOUS INSTRUCTION"

God's child in Christ adopted—Christ my all—
What that earth boasts were not lost cheaply, rather
Than forfeit that blest name, by which I call
The Holy One, the Almighty God, my Father?
Father! in Christ we live, and Christ in Thee—
Eternal Thou, and everlasting we.

WILLIAM LAW (1686-1761)
ENGLISH PROTESTANT CLERGYMAN AND CONTEMPLATIVE
THE SPIRIT OF PRAYER, 1758

All those who follow our Lord Jesus Christ hear the voice of the Father, for it is of them all that the Father says, "These are my chosen sons, in whom I am well pleased."

ST. JOHN OF RUYSBROECK (1293-1381)
FLEMISH MYSTIC

If Jesus is the Son of God, his teachings are more than just good ideas from a wise teacher; they are divine insights on which I can confidently build my life.

LEE STROBEL
AMERICAN JOURNALIST
THE CASE FOR CHRIST, 1998

One of the reasons that Christians read Scripture repeatedly and carefully is to find out just how God works in Jesus Christ so that we can work in the name of Jesus Christ.

EUGENE H. PETERSON
AMERICAN PRESBYTERIAN CHURCH PASTOR AND WRITER
A LONG OBEDIENCE, 1980

They should have known that he was God. His patience should have proved that to them.

TERTULLIAN (C. 160–225)
CHURCH FATHER FROM CARTHAGE

He became what we are that he might make us what he is.

ST. ATHANASIUS (296–373)
BISHOP OF ALEXANDRIA

*W*e believe and know that you are the Holy One of God.

JOHN 6:69

THE LIFE AND TEACHINGS OF JESUS

*B*ut the angel said to them, "Do not be afraid. I bring you good news of great joy that will be for all the people. Today in the town of David a Savior has been born to you; he is Christ the Lord."

LUKE 2:10-11

I have read in Plato and Cicero sayings that are very wise and very beautiful; but I never read in either of them: "Come unto me all ye that labour and are heavy laden."

ST. AUGUSTINE OF HIPPO (354-430)
DOCTOR OF THE CHURCH AND PHILOSOPHER

When we speak about wisdom, we are speaking of Christ. When we speak about virtue, we are speaking of Christ. When we speak about justice, we are speaking of Christ. When we speak about peace, we are speaking of Christ. When we speak about truth and life and redemption, we are speaking of Christ.

ST. AMBROSE (C. 339-397)
BISHOP OF MILAN AND CHURCH FATHER

About this time there lived Jesus, a wise man. . . . He was one who wrought surprising feats and was a teacher of such people as accept the truth gladly. He won over many Jews and many of the Greeks. . . . When Pilate, upon hearing him accused by men of the highest standing amongst us, had condemned him to be crucified, those who had in the first place come to love him did not give up their affection for him. . . . And the tribe of the Christians, so called after him, has still to this day not disappeared.

FLAVIUS JOSEPHUS (C. FIRST CENTURY)
JEWISH HISTORIAN

In the fullness of time Jesus came and taught the reality of the kingdom of God and demonstrated what life could be like in that kingdom. He established a living fellowship that would know him as Redeemer and King, listening to him in all things and obeying him at all times. In his intimate relationship with the father, Jesus modeled for us the reality of that life of hearing and obeying.

RICHARD J. FOSTER
QUAKER THEOLOGIAN, WRITER AND
PROFESSOR OF SPIRITUAL FORMATION
CELEBRATION OF DISCIPLINE, 1978

During the years I have worked with contemporary Jesus research, two words have come to stand out; Jesus as the one who *reveals* and one who *liberates*. Everything that Jesus says and does can be basically described by these two words.

GUSTAF AULEN (1879–1978)
SWEDISH THEOLOGIAN AND BISHOP

The whole of the Old Testament is gathered up in him. He himself embodies in his own person the status and destiny of Israel, and in the community of those who belong to him that status and destiny are to be fulfilled—no longer in the nation as such.

J. W. WENHAM
ANGLICAN NEW TESTAMENT SCHOLAR
CHRIST AND THE BIBLE, 1972

The human life of Jesus, brief and broken as it was,
has realized, once and for all, the truths of eternity.
Jesus of Nazareth gave us by life and teaching, by
death and resurrection, the moral and spiritual
principles which rule the universe of God.

H. WHEELER ROBINSON (1872–1945)
PRINCIPAL, REGENT'S PARK COLLEGE, OXFORD UNIVERSITY
THE CHRISTIAN EXPERIENCE OF THE HOLY SPIRIT, 1928

Jesus, on whom be peace, has said:
The world is a bridge.
Pass over it.
But do not build your dwelling there.

INSCRIPTION AT THE GREAT MOSQUE, FATEH-PUR-SIKRI
(NEAR DELHI, INDIA)

Set before our mind and hearts, O heavenly Father,
the example of our Lord Jesus Christ, who, when he
was upon the earth, found his refreshment in doing
the will of him that sent him, and in
finishing his work.

CHARLES VAUGHAN (1816–1897)
ENGLISH SCHOLAR AND DIVINE

About Jesus we must believe no one but himself.

HENRI FRÉDÉRIC AMIEL (1821–1881)
SWISS CRITIC

This is the will of God which Christ both did and taught: humility in conversation; steadfastness in faith; modesty in words; justice in deeds; mercy in works; discipline in morals; inability to do a wrong, and ability to bear a wrong done; to keep peace with the brethren; to love God with all our hearts; to love Him as a Father; to fear Him as God; to prefer nothing above Christ (because He did not prefer anything above us); to adhere inseparably to His love; and to stand by His cross bravely and faithfully.

ST. CYPRIAN (C. 200-258)
BISHOP OF CARTHAGE AND MARTYR

By His Ascension Our Lord enters heaven and keeps the door open for humanity.

OSWALD CHAMBERS (1874-1917)
SCOTTISH EVANGELIST AND WRITER
MY UTMOST FOR HIS HIGHEST, 1935

Everything Jesus taught revolved around the truth: the truth about the world, the truth about relationships, and the truth about God. The things he taught and the way he taught them set the example for all great teachers who came after him.

BRUCE BICKEL AND STAN JANTZ
WHY JESUS MATTERS, 2003

There are always people who are prepared to pervert the words of Christ for their own purposes, and to deny the final judgment in order to persuade themselves and others that they can sin without fear of punishment. Do not even listen to such people, but turn your back on them.

POLYCARP (C. 69-155)
BISHOP OF SMYRNA
(BURNED AT THE STAKE FOR REFUSING
TO WORSHIP CAESAR AS A GOD)

He said not, "thou shalt not be troubled, thou shalt not be travailed, thou shalt not be diseased;" but He said, "Thou shalt not be overcome."

JULIAN OF NORWICH (C. 1343-1416)
ENGLISH ANCHORESS

When Christ ascended
Triumphantly from star to star
He left the gates of Heaven ajar.

HENRY WADSWORTH LONGFELLOW (1807-1882)
AMERICAN POET
"GOLDEN LEGEND"

What would Jesus do?

CHARLES M. SHELDON (1857-1946)
AMERICAN SOCIAL REFORMER AND PASTOR
IN HIS STEPS, 1899

All four Gospels agree in giving us a picture of a very definite personality. One is obliged to say, "Here was a man. This could not have been invented."

H. G. WELLS (1866-1946)
ENGLISH NOVELIST AND POPULAR HISTORIAN

The raising of Lazarus is the most daring and dramatic of all the Savior's healings. . . .
It was an incredible moment.
It revealed that Jesus was who He said he was—the resurrection and the life. But it revealed something else.
The tears of God.
And who's to say which is more incredible—a man who raises the dead . . . or a God who weeps?

KEN GIRE JR.
MOMENTS WITH THE SAVIOR, 1998

Of all the disciples who floundered and stumbled, Peter was at the forefront. Yet it was to him that Jesus issued that pastoral call: "Feed my sheep."

RAVI ZACHARIAS
INDIAN-BORN THEOLOGIAN AND EVANGELIST

Jesus honored the need for rest. He actually left the needs of people to be quiet in prayer. What the Son of God found necessary should not be neglected by us. Often our most creative times come after a time of resting our minds and bodies. There is an ebb-and-flow rhythm to life in Christ.

LLOYD J. OGILVIE
FORMER CHAPLAIN OF THE U.S. SENATE
GOD'S BEST FOR MY LIFE, 1997

The people who followed Him were unique in their generation. They turned the world upside down because their hearts had been turned right side up. The world has never been the same.

BILLY GRAHAM (WILLIAM FRANKLIN GRAHAM JR.)
AMERICAN EVANGELICAL LEADER AND WRITER
THE SECRET OF HAPPINESS, 1955

Increasingly the gospels are seen as biography . . . four pictures, all different . . . yet all of one and the same man.

RICHARD A. BURRIDGE
ENGLISH DEAN OF KING'S COLLEGE
AND NEW TESTAMENT SCHOLAR

The story of Jesus is the greatest story ever told. It is about the greatest Person who has ever lived. The portrait of Jesus in the Bible reveals God at work in our lives. We see his power. We hear his voice. We experience his love. Jesus towers above the greatest human beings of all time because he is God. . . . When we examine his life, we find ourselves irresistibly drawn to him.

THE KNOWING JESUS STUDY BIBLE, 1999
EDWARD HINDSON AND EDWARD DOBSON, EDS.

The claims of Jesus are so startling that they stop us in our tracks and challenge us to make up our minds about this most remarkable person. Was He just a great teacher? Or was He much more?

MICHAEL GREEN
BRITISH THEOLOGIAN AND EVANGELIST
WHO IS THIS JESUS? 1992

No one can read the Gospels without feeling the actual presence of Jesus. His personality pulsates in every word.

ALBERT EINSTEIN (1879-1955)
GERMAN-BORN THEORETICAL PHYSICIST
AND NOBEL PRIZE WINNER

Surely one of the most powerful lines in the Bible is one of the simplest: "Jesus wept."

MARIANNE WILLIAMSON
AMERICAN SPIRITUAL LECTURER AND WRITER
EVERYDAY GRACE, 2002

We believe in one God, the Father, all sovereign, the Maker of things visible and invisible; and in one Lord Jesus Christ, the Word of God, God of God, Light of Light, Son only-begotten, Firstborn of all Creation, begotten of the Father before all ages, through whom also all things were made; who was made flesh for our salvation and lived among men, and suffered, and rose again on the third day, and ascended to the Father, who shall come again in glory to judge the living and the dead.

EUSEBIUS OF CAESAREA (C. 260-341)
THEOLOGIAN AND "FATHER OF CHURCH HISTORY"
COUNCIL OF NICEA, 325

That a few simple men should in one generation have invented so powerful and appealing a personality, so lofty an ethic, and so inspiring a vision of human brotherhood, would be a miracle far more incredible than any recorded in the Gospels.

WILL DURANT (WILLIAM JAMES DURANT) (1885-1981)
AMERICAN HISTORIAN AND PHILOSOPHER

Christ cannot be separated from the miraculous; His birth, His ministrations and His resurrection, all involve the miraculous, and the change which His religion works in the human heart is a continuing miracle.

WILLIAM JENNINGS BRYAN (1860–1925)
DEMOCRATIC POLITICIAN AND POPULIST
THE PRINCE OF PEACE, 1909

No teacher ever showed more belief than our Lord in the capacity of the ordinary man to think rightly, if he be only sincere and open-minded. He did not, except rarely, use the dogmatic method. It would seem as if He feared to stunt men's growth from within thereby.

CHARLES GORE (1853–1932)
ENGLISH BISHOP AND THEOLOGIAN
A NEW COMMENTARY ON HOLY SCRIPTURE, 1928

Many facts about Jesus are attractive to the secular mind. He exhibited a gentle spirit and showed great compassion for the poor and hurting. He continually called for justice to be balanced with mercy. His radical teachings were completely opposite of the counsel of others: Rather than advocating revenge, Jesus taught people to love their neighbors in the same way in which they loved themselves.

But there is one claim about Jesus that is highly offensive to our pluralistic society: the truth that faith in him is the *only* way to heaven.

THE KNOWING JESUS STUDY BIBLE, 1999
EDWARD HINDSON AND EDWARD DOBSON, EDS.
(BIBLICAL REFERENCES DELETED FROM EXCERPT)

I hold the precepts of Jesus, as delivered by Himself, to be the most pure, benevolent and sublime which have ever been preached to man. . . .

THOMAS JEFFERSON (1743-1826)
U.S. PRESIDENT AND STATESMAN

Christ is born: glorify him. Christ comes from heaven: go out to meet him. Christ descends to earth: let us be raised on high.

ST. GREGORY OF NAZIANZUS (c. 330-390)
CAPPADOCIAN CHURCH FATHER

Christ appeared not as a philosopher or wordy doctor, or noisy disputer, or even as a wise and learned scribe, but he talked with people in complete simplicity, showing them the way of the truth in the way he lived, his goodness and his miracles.

ANGELA OF FOLIGNO (1248-1309)
ITALIAN MYSTIC

In all your deeds and words, you should look on
Jesus as your model, whether you are keeping silence
or speaking, whether you are alone or with others.

ST. BONAVENTURE (1221-1274)
TUSCAN-BORN FRANCISCAN THEOLOGIAN

In your reading, let not your end be to seek and find
out curiosities and subtleties, but to find
and meet with Christ.

THOMAS TAYLOR (1576-1633)
ENGLISH PURITAN THEOLOGIAN

Help me to receive faith from his miraculous
conception, humility from his lowly birth, patience
from his suffering, power to crucify the sin in my life
from his Cross, burial of all my evil thoughts in good
works from his burial. Grant that I might be able to
meditate on hell from his descent, to find newness
of life in his resurrection, to set my mind on things
above from his ascension, to judge myself in
preparation of his returning judgment.

BISHOP LANCELOT ANDREWES (1555-1626)
ENGLISH PREACHER AND WRITER OF SERMONS
PRIVATE DEVOTIONS

Christ's character was more wonderful than
the greatest miracle.

ALFRED LORD TENNYSON (1809-1892)
ENGLISH POET

"Lord, teach us to pray." Ah! If we were only
convinced of our ignorance and of our need of a
Teacher like Jesus Christ! If we would only approach
him with confidence, asking him to teach us himself
and desiring to be taught by his grace how to
converse with God! How soon we should be skilled
in it and how many of his secrets we
should discover!

JEAN-NICOLAS GROU (1731-1803)
FRENCH JESUIT PRIEST
THE SCHOOL OF JESUS CHRIST, 1932

Identifying Jesus primarily through what he does,
says, and suffers, is set within the larger story of God
in relation to Israel, and Jewish Scriptures and
traditions are pervasively important in
describing him.

OXFORD READERS: JESUS, 2002
DAVID F. FORD AND MIKE HIGTON, EDS.

The teaching of Jesus astonished and delighted all the people, because it promised liberty to all. The teaching of Jesus was the fulfillment of the prophesies of Isaiah, that the chosen of God should bring light unto men, should defeat evil, and should establish truth, not by violence, but by mildness, humility, and goodness.

LEO TOLSTOY (1828-1910)
RUSSIAN NOVELIST
THE SPIRIT OF CHRIST'S TEACHING, 1899

The Sermon on the Mount is Christ's biography. Every syllable He had already written down in deeds. The sermon merely translated His life into language.

THOMAS WRIGHT (1810-1877)
ENGLISH QUAKER ANTIQUARY

The highest service may be prepared for and done in the humblest surroundings. In silence, in waiting, in obscure, unnoticed offices, in years of uneventful, unrecorded duties, the Son of God grew and waxed strong.

INSCRIPTION IN THE CHAPEL OF STANFORD UNIVERSITY
PALO ALTO, CALIFORNIA

Christ's outwardly life was one of the most troubled
lives that was ever lived: tempest and tumult, tumult
and tempest, the waves breaking over it all the time.
But the inner life was a sea of glass. The great
calm was always there.

HENRY DRUMMOND (1851-1897)
SCOTTISH PREACHER AND EVANGELIST

Everything that happened to Christ lets us know
that, after the washing of water, the Holy Spirit
descends upon us from the heights of heaven, and
that we become sons of God, having been adopted
by the voice of the Father.

HILARY OF POITIERS (FOURTH CENTURY)
BISHOP OF POITIERS AND THEOLOGIAN

It is Christianity's most irreducible tenet: On the
third day, Jesus rose from the grave. From the very
beginning Christians have proclaimed the
Resurrection a validation of all that Jesus taught and
all they believe him to be. It is the foundation
upon which all else rests.

JEFFREY L. SHELER
"THE LAST DAYS OF JESUS"
U.S. NEWS & WORLD REPORT SPECIAL EDITION:
MYSTERIES OF FAITH, JAN. 2004

The miracles of Jesus are in keeping with reality. They do not appear as the fantasies of the imagination. Rather, they are presented as serious historical events which we might expect to occur if a supernatural God were attempting to verify a truth by breaking into the natural order.

JOSH MCDOWELL
AMERICAN THEOLOGIAN AND YOUTH LEADER

The demands of Jesus are difficult just because they require us to do something extraordinary. At the same time he asks us to regard these as something usual, ordinary.

ALBERT SCHWEITZER (1875–1965)
ALSACE-BORN MUSICIAN, NEW TESTAMENT SCHOLAR,
MEDICAL MISSIONARY AND NOBEL PEACE PRIZE WINNER
SERMON ON REVERENCE FOR LIFE, 1919

The claim that God raised Jesus from the grave is so stupendous that no one could be expected to believe it without very strong evidence. Yet without the resurrection, there would have been no gospel, no Christian faith, no church and no New Testament.

SIR NORMAN ANDERSON (1908–1994)
ENGLISH PROFESSOR OF LAW

'Twas a thief said the last kind word to Christ:
Christ took the kindness and forgave the theft.

ROBERT BROWNING (1812-1889)
ENGLISH POET

Jesus' acts of healing and exorcism formed the major
part of his activity and made the greatest impression
upon those around him. . . . The healings and
exorcisms were not simply remarkable cures of
physical disorders but the means by which individual
men and women received the kingdom, brought to
them in the person of Jesus, with the consequence
that their whole existence was transformed and the
reign of God become a reality in their lives.

J. R. PORTER DUNCAN
ENGLISH PROFESSOR OF THEOLOGY
JESUS CHRIST: THE JESUS OF HISTORY,
THE CHRIST OF FAITH, 1999

Jesus did not say—Make converts to your way of
thinking, but look after My sheep, see that they get
nourished in the knowledge of Me. . . . Discipleship
is based on devotion to Jesus Christ, not on
adherence to a belief or a creed.

OSWALD CHAMBERS (1874-1917)
SCOTTISH EVANGELIST AND WRITER
MY UTMOST FOR HIS HIGHEST, 1935

Jesus was Himself the One convincing and
permanent miracle.

IAN MACLAREN (1850–1907)
(PSEUDONYM FOR REV. JOHN WATSON)
SCOTTISH AUTHOR AND DIVINE

Jesus (literally "one who saves"). The man born in
Bethlehem and brought up in Nazareth who became
an itinerant teacher, was crucified and rose again.
His followers came to believe he was the Messiah
(Christ) and the Son of God.

AN INTRODUCTION TO THE CHRISTIAN FAITH, 1982
(GLOSSARY)
ROBIN KEELEY, ED.

His words are the essence of truth. . . . Jesus never
uttered opinions. He never guessed; He knew,
and He knows.

A. W. TOZER (AIDEN WILSON TOZER) (1897–1963)
AMERICAN PASTOR AND WRITER

———◆◆◆———

To this end I was born, and for this cause came I into the world,
that I should bear witness unto the truth.

JOHN 18:37 (KJV)

THE LOVE OF CHRIST

A new command I give you: Love one another. As I have loved you, so you must love one another. By this all men will know that you are my disciples, if you love one another.

JOHN 13:34-35

They are the true disciples of Christ, not who know most, but who love most.

FREDERICK SPANHEIM THE ELDER (1600-1649)
DUTCH THEOLOGIAN

I believe there is nothing lovelier, deeper, more sympathetic and more perfect than the Saviour; I say to myself with jealous love that not only is there no one else like Him, but that there could be no one.

FYODOR DOSTOEVSKY (1821-1881)
RUSSIAN WRITER
THE BROTHERS KARAMAZOV, 1879

What can I give Him,
Poor as I am?
If I were a shepherd,
I would bring a lamb;
If I were a Wise Man,
I would do my part;
Yet what can I give Him?
—Give my heart.

CHRISTINA ROSSETTI (1830–1894)
ENGLISH POET
"MID-WINTER," 1875

Late have I loved you, O beauty ancient and so new. Late have I loved you! You were within me while I have gone outside to seek you. Unlovely myself, I rushed towards all those lovely things you had made. And always you were with me, and I was not with you. . . . You touched me, and now I burn with longing for your peace.

ST. AUGUSTINE OF HIPPO (354–430)
DOCTOR OF THE CHURCH AND PHILOSOPHER
CONFESSIONS, 398

There are three central aspects of Christianity. The first is the hope of eternal life, which is the beginning and end of our faith. The second is righteousness, which is the beginning and end of judgment. The third is joy, which is the beginning and end of love. Through the resurrection of Jesus Christ, we have had a glimpse of what is promised for all who are saved, because he is the first fruits of the harvest of salvation. Through the example of Jesus Christ in his life and work, we understand righteousness, and by following his example we can be sure of favorable judgment. Through the joy that Jesus mediates, which originates in his perfect heart of love, we want to share that joy and so grow in his love.

"THE EPISTLE OF BARNABAS"
(C. EARLY SECOND CENTURY)

He who truly possesses the words of Jesus Christ in his heart hears those words constantly within the silence of his heart; and his every action expresses Christ's love.

IGNATIUS OF ANTIOCH (C. SECOND CENTURY)
BISHOP OF ANTIOCH IN SYRIA
(ON THE EPISTLE TO THE EPHESIANS)

"How much do you love me?" I asked Jesus, and Jesus said, "This much. . . ." Then he stretched out his arms and died.

AUTHOR UNKNOWN

Jesus loves the little children,
All the children of the world.
Red and yellow, black and white,
They are precious in his sight.
Jesus loves the little children of the world.

CLARE HERBERT WOOLSTON (NINETEENTH CENTURY)
AMERICAN PREACHER
SUNDAY SCHOOL SONG

One who is safe and secure in the love of God and
sustained by His grace no longer hears from a distant
God. He now listens to Someone who loves him
enough to bring him to a personal relationship,
and that makes all the difference.

CHARLES STANLEY
AMERICAN BAPTIST PASTOR AND BROADCASTER
HOW TO LISTEN TO GOD, 1985

Jesus, Thou Joy of loving hearts,
Thou Fount of Life, Thou Light of men,
From the best bliss that earth imparts
We turn unfilled to Thee again.

ST. BERNARD OF CLAIRVAUX (1091–1153)
FRENCH MONK AND FOUNDER OF THE CISTERCIAN ORDER

O Christ, my Master and Lord,
grant that I may know thee more clearly,
love thee more dearly,
follow thee more nearly,
day by day.

RICHARD OF CHICHESTER (1197–1253)
ENGLISH BISHOP

The love of Jesus is not mere sentiment; it is
active and energetic.

CHARLES HADDON SPURGEON (1834–1892)
ENGLISH NONCONFORMIST PREACHER

What could be greater than to be seen doing the
things of Christ declared to be proofs
of love for Him?

ST. JOHN CHRYSOSTOM (C. 347–407)
ARCHBISHOP OF CONSTANTINOPLE AND CHURCH FATHER

Contemplate the Love of Christ, and you will love.
Stand before that mirror, reflect Christ's character,
and you will be changed into the same image from
tenderness to tenderness. There is no other way.

HENRY DRUMMOND (1851–1897)
SCOTTISH PREACHER AND EVANGELIST
THE GREATEST THING IN THE WORLD, 1890

Do not fill your head with complex theories about God and the heavens, because no human ideas can permeate the divine mystery; God has revealed enough of himself for each of us to love him with all our hearts.

SHEPHERD OF HERMAS (C. SECOND CENTURY)
APOSTOLIC FATHER AND CHURCH WRITER

Then, O then, I heard a voice which said, "There is one, even Christ Jesus, that can speak to thy condition"; and when I heard it my heart did leap for joy . . . and then the Lord did gently lead me along and did let me see His love, which was endless and eternal and surpasseth all the knowledge that men have in the natural state or can get by history or books.

GEORGE FOX (1624–1691)
ENGLISH FOUNDER OF
THE SOCIETY OF FRIENDS (THE QUAKERS)
JOURNAL

Celebration is at the heart of the way of Christ.

RICHARD J. FOSTER
QUAKER THEOLOGIAN, WRITER AND
PROFESSOR OF SPIRITUAL FORMATION
CELEBRATION OF DISCIPLINE, 1978

If we truly love Christ, we shall care for those
who are loved by Him.

CHARLES HADDON SPURGEON (1834-1892)
ENGLISH NONCONFORMIST PREACHER

The central message of the New Testament is that
there is really only one prayer and that is the prayer
of Christ. It is a prayer that continues in our hearts
day and night. It is the stream of love that flows
constantly between Jesus and his Father. It is the
Holy Spirit. It is the most important task of any fully
human life to become as open as possible
to this stream of love.

JOHN MAIN
ENGLISH BENEDICTINE MONK
MOMENT OF CHRIST, 1984

The ground of our hope is Christ in the world, but
the evidence of our hope is Christ in the heart.

MATTHEW HENRY (1662-1714)
ENGLISH BIBLE COMMENTATOR

Live in Christ's love while ye are here,
and all the way.

SAMUEL RUTHERFORD (C. 1600-1661)
SCOTTISH PRESBYTERIAN MINISTER

We are alone when we enter the world, but when we leave it we shall feel the abiding presence of the Lord. As death draws near and we dread the dark journey ahead, the Lord will assure us that our lives are precious in the sight of God. He will gently say, "Child, come home." Jesus has given his word that he will never leave us or forsake us, and his word is as firm as his character.

EDWARD JOHN CARNELL (1919-1967)
PRESIDENT OF FULLER SEMINARY AND EVANGELICAL TEACHER

The secret of life in Christ is challenging: do the thing that love demands and you will feel the love that the thing requires.

LLOYD J. OGILVIE
FORMER CHAPLAIN OF THE U.S. SENATE
GOD'S BEST FOR MY LIFE, 1997

O Love that wilt not let me go,
I rest my weary soul in thee;
I give thee back the life I owe,
That in thine ocean depths its flow
may richer, fuller be.

GEORGE MATHESON (1842-1906)
SCOTTISH MINISTER
HYMN, "O LOVE THAT WILT NOT LET ME GO," 1882

Learn then from Christ, O Christian, how Christ should be loved. Learn to love Him tenderly, prudently, and with all thy might.

ST. BERNARD OF CLAIRVAUX (1091–1153)
FRENCH MONK AND FOUNDER OF THE CISTERCIAN ORDER
SERMON ON THE SONG OF SONGS

Christianity taught men that love is worth more than intelligence.

JACQUES MARITAIN (1882–1973)
FRENCH PHILOSOPHER

Every act of kindness and compassion done by any man for his fellow Christian is done by Christ working within him.

JULIAN OF NORWICH (C. 1343–1416)
ENGLISH ANCHORESS

He who begins by loving Christianity better than truth will proceed by loving his own sect or church better than Christianity and end in loving himself better than all.

SAMUEL TAYLOR COLERIDGE (1772–1834)
ENGLISH POET AND LITERARY CRITIC

What is Christian perfection? Loving God with all
our heart, mind, soul and strength.

JOHN WESLEY (1703–1791)
ENGLISH PREACHER AND FOUNDER OF METHODISM

Tell me the old, old story
Of unseen things above,
Of Jesus and His glory
Of Jesus and His love.

A. CATHERINE HANKEY (1834–1911)
BRITISH HYMN WRITER
HYMN, "TELL ME THE OLD, OLD STORY"

Our redemption through the suffering of Christ is
that deeper love within us which not only frees us
from slavery to sin, but also secures for us the true
liberty of the children of God, in order that we might
do all things out of love rather than out of fear—love
for him who has shown us such grace that no
greater grace can be found.

PETER ABELARD (1079–1142)
FRENCH PHILOSOPHER AND THEOLOGIAN
COMMENTARY ON ROMANS

The only way to deliver me from my self-
centeredness is by winning my entire heart's
devotion, the total allegiance of my will to God—and

this can only be done by the Divine Love of God disclosed by Christ in his life and death.

WILLIAM TEMPLE (1881–1944)
ANGLICAN ARCHBISHOP OF CANTERBURY AND WRITER

Christian perfection is not so severe, tiresome, and constraining as we think. It asks us to be God's from the bottom of our hearts. And since we thus are God's, everything that we do for him is easy.

FRANÇOIS FÉNELON (1651–1715)
FRENCH ARCHBISHOP
CHRISTIAN PERFECTION, 1947

To Jesus religion was *service*. It was love of God *and* love of men. Ritual was irrelevant compared with love in action. To Jesus the most important thing in the world was not the correct performance of a ritual, but the spontaneous answer to the cry of human need.

WILLIAM BARCLAY
SCOTTISH THEOLOGIAN, RELIGIOUS WRITER AND
BROADCASTER

Above all the grace and the gifts that Christ gives to His beloved is that of overcoming self.

ST. FRANCIS OF ASSISI (1182–1226)
ITALIAN FOUNDER OF THE FRANCISCAN ORDER

How sweet the name of Jesus sounds
In a believer's ear!

JOHN NEWTON (1725–1807)
EVANGELICAL HYMN WRITER AND FORMER SLAVE TRADER
HYMN, "THE NAME OF JESUS"

Many people mistake our work for our vocation.
Our vocation is the love of Jesus.

MOTHER TERESA (AGNES GONXHA BOJAXHIU)
(1910–1997)
ALBANIAN-BORN CATHOLIC MISSIONARY
AND NOBEL PEACE PRIZE WINNER
NEW YORK TIMES, 1986

I am nothing, I have nothing. I desire nothing but
the love of Jesus in Jerusalem.

WALTER HILTON (FOURTEENTH CENTURY)
ENGLISH SPIRITUAL WRITER AND AUGUSTINIAN CANON
THE SCALE OF PERFECTION

How do I love thee? Let me count the ways.
I love thee to the depth and breadth and height
My soul can reach, when feeling out of sight
For the ends of being and of ideal Grace.

ELIZABETH BARRETT BROWNING (1806–1861)
ENGLISH POET
SONNETS FROM THE PORTUGUESE
"MY CHILDHOOD FAITH," 1850

In every pang that rends the heart
The Man of Sorrow had a part.

MICHAEL BRUCE (1746-1767)
SCOTTISH POET

In the greatest showing of love imaginable, Christ
came into human life, into the story that love had
made, as Jesus of Nazareth. Christ, the Second
Person of the Trinity, left the place of Creation and
power and became mortal, open to temptation, to
weakness and fatigue, to sorrow and joy,
and laughter and tears.

MADELEINE L'ENGLE
AMERICAN AWARD-WINNING WRITER

Jesus, confirm my heart's desire,
To work, and speak, and think for thee,
Still let me guard the holy fire,
And still stir up thy gift in me.

Ready for all thy perfect will,
My acts of faith and love repeat,
Till death thy endless mercies seal,
And make the sacrifice complete.

CHARLES WESLEY (1707-1788)
ENGLISH METHODIST PREACHER AND HYMN WRITER
HYMN, "O THOU WHO COMEST FROM ABOVE"

There is but one love of Jesus, as there is but one person in the poor—Jesus. We take vows of chastity to love Christ with undivided love; to be able to love him with undivided love we take a vow of poverty which frees us from all material possessions, and with that freedom we can love him with undivided love, and from this vow of undivided love we surrender ourselves totally to him in the person who takes his place.

MOTHER TERESA (AGNES GONXHA BOJAXHIU)
(1910-1997)
ALBANIAN-BORN CATHOLIC MISSIONARY
AND NOBEL PEACE PRIZE WINNER
A GIFT FOR GOD, 1975

If ever you should doubt the love of God, take a long, deep look at the cross, for in the cross you find the expression of God's love.

BILLY GRAHAM (WILLIAM FRANKLIN GRAHAM JR.)
AMERICAN EVANGELICAL LEADER AND WRITER
PEACE WITH GOD, 1953

The mysterious growth of Jesus Christ in our heart is the accomplishment of God's purpose, the fruit of his grace and divine will.

JEAN-PIERRE DE CAUSSADE (1675-1751)
FRENCH JESUIT PRIEST AND ASCETIC WRITER

Consider the mysteries of love, and you will then
have a vision of the bosom of the Father, whom the
only-begotten God alone has declared. God himself is
love, and for the sake of this love he has
made himself known.

ST. CLEMENT OF ALEXANDRIA (C. 150-215)
GREEK THEOLOGIAN AND CHURCH FATHER
ON THE RICH MAN'S SALVATION

I am convinced that neither death nor life, neither angels nor demons, neither the present nor the future, nor any powers, neither height nor depth, nor anything else in all creation, will be able to separate us from the love of God that is in Christ Jesus our Lord.

ROMANS 8:38-39

LIFE IN CHRIST

Therefore, if anyone is in Christ, he is a new creation; the old has gone, the new has come!

2 CORINTHIANS 5:17

I have a great need for Christ; I have a great Christ for my need.

CHARLES HADDON SPURGEON (1834–1892)
ENGLISH NONCONFORMIST PREACHER

What does the divine sufferer demand from us? Only our faith, our love, our grateful praise, our consecrated hearts and lives. Is that too much to ask?

BILLY GRAHAM (WILLIAM FRANKLIN GRAHAM JR.)
AMERICAN EVANGELICAL LEADER AND WRITER

When Christ came into my life, I came about like
a well-handled ship.

ROBERT LOUIS STEVENSON (1850-1894)
SCOTTISH NOVELIST

It is from within the place of prayer, recollection,
worship and love, where the altar is, where the
sacrifice is made, where we are all bound together
in a life of communion and self-giving to God, that
we fully and truly receive the revelation which
is made through Christ.

EVELYN UNDERHILL (1875-1941)
ENGLISH SPIRITUAL WRITER
LIGHT OF CHRIST, 1944

Awake, then, thou that sleepest, and Christ, who
from all eternity has been espoused to thy soul, shall
give thee light. Begin to search and dig in thine own
field for this pearl of eternity that lies hidden in it; it
cannot cost thee too much, nor canst thou buy it too
dear, for it is *all;* and when thou hast found it thou
wilt know all which thou hast sold or given away for
it as mere a nothing as a bubble upon the water.

WILLIAM LAW (1686-1761)
ENGLISH PROTESTANT CONTEMPLATIVE AND CLERIC
THE SPIRIT OF PRAYER, 1758

How else but through a broken heart
May Lord Christ enter in?

OSCAR WILDE (1854–1900)
ANGLO-IRISH DRAMATIST AND POET
"THE BALLAD OF READING GAOL," 1898

The perfect surrender and humiliation were
undergone by Christ: perfect because He was God,
surrender and humiliation because He was man. . . .
In Christ a new kind of man appeared: and the new
kind of life which began in Him is to be put into us.

C. S. LEWIS (CLIVE STAPLES LEWIS) (1898–1963)
IRISH LITERARY SCHOLAR,
CHRISTIAN APOLOGIST AND WRITER
MERE CHRISTIANITY, 1943

Some events stand out as events of God's acting, for
these events have the power to address men at the
deepest level of their existence, to seize them, as it
were, and bring them into the attitude of faith. . . .
The event of Jesus Christ is, for Christians, the
supreme miracle, the high tide of God's
providential activity.

JOHN MACQUARRIE
SCOTTISH THEOLOGIAN
PRINCIPLES OF CHRISTIAN THEOLOGY, 1977

Those who know God in Christ have found the
secret of true freedom and true humanity.

JAMES I. PACKER
BRITISH EVANGELICAL THEOLOGIAN AND WRITER
KNOWING GOD, 1993

Then, as now, it was the truth *of* Jesus, and not the
truth *about* Jesus, which convinced and
converted. . . . No words can add to the Word.

JOHN V. TAYLOR
ANGLICAN BISHOP OF WINCHESTER
THE GO-BETWEEN GOD, 1972

Jesus' force resides in his vulnerability not only on
the cross but throughout his life. He entices each of
us to meet him in that dangerous place where an
awareness of our own weakness and fragility shatters
the self and blossoms into an image of
God within us.

BRUCE CHILTON
PROFESSOR OF RELIGION
RABBI JESUS: AN INTIMATE BIOGRAPHY, 2000

Settle yourself in solitude and you will come upon
Him in yourself.

ST. TERESA OF AVILA (1515–1582)
SPANISH CARMELITE NUN AND MYSTIC

The believer who studies this life of Christ as the pattern and the promise of what his may be, learns to understand how the "Without me ye can do nothing" is but the forerunner of "I can do all things through Christ who strengtheneth me."

ANDREW MURRAY (1828-1917)
PREACHER AND AUTHOR IN SOUTH AFRICA AND SCOTLAND
"AS CHRIST IN THE FATHER"

In a deep and real sense, Christ is the one answer to our many questions, and we gain that answer by the experience of Him, not by a number of statements about him. He becomes to us the centre of life, because our life finds its only satisfaction in Him, and then, as we interpret life from this new experience.

H. WHEELER ROBINSON (1872-1945)
PRINCIPAL, REGENT'S PARK COLLEGE, OXFORD UNIVERSITY
THE CHRISTIAN EXPERIENCE OF THE HOLY SPIRIT, 1928

Begin at once; before you venture away from this quiet moment, ask your King to take you wholly into His service, and place all the hours of this day quite simply at His disposal, and ask Him to make and keep you ready to do just exactly what he appoints.

FRANCES RIDLEY HAVERGAL (1836-1879)
ENGLISH POET AND HYMN WRITER

Every thought we think, in every hour we live, must be, not necessarily about Christ, but it must be the thought Christ would think were he placed in our circumstances and subject to our conditions.

HANNAH WHITALL SMITH (1832–1911)
QUAKER EVANGELIST
THE CHRISTIAN'S SECRET OF A HAPPY LIFE, 1870

He who does not long to know more of Christ, knows nothing of him yet.

CHARLES HADDON SPURGEON (1834–1892)
ENGLISH NONCONFORMIST PREACHER

He came to those men who knew him not. He speaks to us the same word: "Follow thou me!" and sets us to the tasks which he has to fulfill for our time. He commands. And to those who obey him, he will reveal himself in the toils, the conflicts, the sufferings which they shall pass through in his fellowship, and, as an ineffable mystery, they shall learn in their own experience who he is.

ALBERT SCHWEITZER (1875–1965)
ALSACE-BORN MUSICIAN, NEW TESTAMENT SCHOLAR,
MEDICAL MISSIONARY AND NOBEL PEACE PRIZE WINNER

Christ be with me, Christ within me,
Christ behind me, Christ before me,
Christ beside me, Christ to win me,
Christ to comfort and restore me,
Christ beneath me, Christ above me,
Christ in quiet, Christ in danger,
Christ in hearts of all that love me,
Christ in mouth of friend and stranger.

PRAYER ATTRIBUTED TO ST. PATRICK (C. 390-460)
PATRON SAINT AND APOSTLE OF IRELAND

O blessed Jesus, give me stillness of soul in thee.
Let thy mighty calmness reign in me;
Rule me, O King of gentleness, King of peace.

ST. JOHN OF THE CROSS (1542-1591)
SPANISH CARMELITE PRIEST AND MYSTIC

The touch of Christ sanctifies all the sufferings and
sorrows of those who believe in Him.

MARTIN LUTHER (1485-1546)
GERMAN MONK, THEOLOGIAN
AND LEADER OF THE PROTESTANT REFORMATION
"THAT A CHRISTIAN SHOULD BEAR
HIS CROSS WITH PATIENCE"

Dear Jesus, help us to spread your fragrance
everywhere we go. Flood our souls with your spirit
and life. Penetrate and possess our whole being so
utterly that our lives may only be a radiance of yours.
Shine through us, and be so in us, that every soul we
come in contact with may feel your presence
in our soul.

JOHN HENRY NEWMAN (1801–1890)
ENGLISH CARDINAL AND LEADER OF THE OXFORD MOVEMENT

We remain in Christ by communicating with him,
doing what he says, living by faith, and relating in
love to the community of believers.
So stay close, be nourished, and bear fruit.

DAVID VEERMAN
BESIDE STILL WATERS, 1996

Our confidence in Christ does not make us lazy,
negligent, or careless, but on the contrary it awakens
us, urges us on, and makes us active in living
righteous lives and doing good. There is no
self-confidence to compare with this.

ULRICH ZWINGLI (1484–1531)
FOUNDER OF SWISS PROTESTANTISM

The second greatest miracle, next to Christ, is what happens to a person who comes to know Christ personally. When we commit our lives to Him and invite Him to live in us, our days are filled with a constant succession of surprises. He is Lord of all life, has unlimited power, and can arrange events and circumstances to bless us. Our only task is to surrender our needs to Him, and then leave the results to Him.

LLOYD J. OGILVIE
FORMER CHAPLAIN OF THE U.S. SENATE
GOD'S BEST FOR MY LIFE, 1997

Do little things as if they were great, because of the majesty of the Lord Jesus Christ who dwells in thee; and do great things as if they were little and easy, because of his omnipotence.

BLAISE PASCAL (1623-1662)
FRENCH PHILOSOPHER, MATHEMATICIAN AND PHYSICIST

Not what, but whom!
For Christ is more than all the creeds,
And His full life of gentle deeds
Shall all the creeds outlive.
Not what I do believe but whom!
Who walks beside me in the gloom?

Who shares the burden wearisome?
Who all the dim way doth illume,
And bids me look beyond the tomb
The larger life to live?
Not what I do believe
But whom!
Not what but whom!

JOHN OXENHAM (1852–1941)
(PSEUDONYM FOR WILLIAM ARTHUR DUNKERLEY)
BRITISH JOURNALIST, NOVELIST AND POET
"BEES IN AMBER," 1913

The Christian life begins with an encounter with
Jesus Christ. It cannot be otherwise. . . . Many
influences and experiences may lead us to an
encounter with Jesus Christ. Those influences and
experiences may even be intensely religious and
theologically profound—but until a person responds
to the promise of Christ and receives Him as Lord,
there can be no spiritual reality, nor eternal life.

RAY C. STEDMAN (1917–1992)
AMERICAN PASTOR AND PREACHER
AUTHENTIC CHRISTIANITY, 1966

Peace of the running waves to you,
Deep peace of the flowing air to you,
Deep peace of the quiet earth to you,
Deep peace of the shining stars to you,
Deep peace of the shades of night to you,
Moon and stars always giving light to you,
Deep peace of Christ, the Son of Peace, to you.

AUTHOR UNKNOWN
CELTIC PRAYER, CITED IN *THE DOUBLEDAY CHRISTIAN*
QUOTATION BOOK, 1997

I grasped that over it lay, as it were, a cable-bridge,
frail, swaying, but passable. And this bridge, this
reconciliation between the black despair of lying
bound and gagged in the tiny dungeon of ego, and
soaring upwards into the white radiance of God's
universal love—this bridge was the Incarnation,
whose truth expresses that of the desperate need it
meets. Because of our physical hunger we know there
is bread; because of our spiritual hunger
we know there is Christ.

MALCOLM MUGGERIDGE (1903–1990)
BRITISH JOURNALIST AND MAGAZINE EDITOR
THE GREEN STICK, 1972

Every step toward Christ kills doubt. Every thought,
word and deed for Him carries you away
from discouragement.

THEODORE LEDYARD CUYLER (1822–1909)
AMERICAN PRESBYTERIAN CLERGYMAN AND WRITER

God speaks sometimes through our circumstances
and guides us, closing doors as well as opening them.
He will let you know what you must do, and what
you must be. He is waiting for you to touch Him.
The hand of faith is enough. Your trembling fingers
can reach Him as He passes. Reach out your faith—
touch Him. He will not ask, "who touched me?"
He will know.

PETER MARSHALL SR.
FORMER CHAPLAIN OF THE U.S. SENATE
"THE TOUCH OF FAITH," RADIO BROADCAST SERMON, 1949

True Christianity is an all-out commitment
to Jesus Christ.

JOHN FLAVEL (C. 1639–1691)
ENGLISH PRESBYTERIAN MINISTER

I believe Plato and Socrates. I believe in Jesus Christ.

SAMUEL TAYLOR COLERIDGE (1772–1834)
ENGLISH POET AND LITERARY CRITIC

When people find out that you are a Christian, they should already have an idea of who you are and what you are like simply because you bear such a precious name.

JONI EARECKSON TADA
FOUNDER OF JONI AND FRIENDS MINISTRY

Apart from Christ we know neither what our life nor death is; we do not know what God is nor what we ourselves are.

BLAISE PASCAL (1623–1662)
FRENCH PHILOSOPHER, MATHEMATICIAN AND PHYSICIST
PENSÉES, PUBLISHED POSTHUMOUSLY

Christ stimulates us, as other great men stimulate us, but we find a power coming from Him into our lives that enables us to respond. That is the experience that proves Him to be the universal Spirit. It does not happen with others.

WILLIAM TEMPLE (1881–1944)
ANGLICAN ARCHBISHOP OF CANTERBURY AND WRITER

We should live our lives as though Christ was coming this afternoon.

JIMMY CARTER (JAMES EARL CARTER)
U.S. PRESIDENT AND DIPLOMAT

Have we opened our door to Christ? Have we ever invited him in? That was exactly the question I needed to have put to me. For, intellectually speaking, I had believed in Jesus all my life, on the other side of the door. . . . But all the time, often without realizing it, I was holding Christ at arm's length and keeping him outside. I knew that to open the door might have momentous consequences.

JOHN R. W. STOTT
RECTOR EMERITUS OF ALL SOULS CHURCH, LONDON
CHRISTIAN BASICS, 1991

Christ himself came down and took possession of me. In my arguments about the insolubility of God I had never foreseen the possibility of that, of a real contact, person to person, here below, between a human being and God.

SIMONE WEIL (1909–1943)
FRENCH PHILOSOPHER AND POLITICAL ACTIVIST
QUOTED IN *ATTENTE DE DIEU*, 1969

Every sermon should be an agony of the soul, a passion to beget Christ in the souls of men.

ST. JOHN CHRYSOSTOM (C. 347–407)
ARCHBISHOP OF CONSTANTINOPLE AND CHURCH FATHER

Relationship with Jesus is the origin, motivation, and goal of the Christian faith. This requires belief that Jesus Christ is alive, that he is divine, and that he is still inviting us to fellowship with him.

LUIS PALAU
ARGENTINE-BORN EVANGELICAL PREACHER

Of all the traits of a life like Christ, there is none higher and more glorious than conformity to Him in the work that now engages Him without ceasing in the Father's presence: His all-powerful intercession. The more we abide in Him and grow more like Him, the more His priestly life will work in us. Our lives will become what His is—a life that continuously prays for men.

ANDREW MURRAY (1828-1917)
PREACHER AND AUTHOR IN SOUTH AFRICA AND SCOTLAND
"WITH CHRIST IN THE SCHOOL OF PRAYER"

To be in Christ is the source of the Christian's life; to be like Christ is the sum of his excellence; to be with Christ is the fullness of his joy.

CHARLES HODGE (1797-1878)
PROFESSOR AT PRINCETON THEOLOGICAL SEMINARY

Let the people of God acknowledge that they are a new creation in Jesus Christ, and with souls on the watch, understand by whom they have been assumed and whom they have assumed.

POPE LEO I (FIFTH CENTURY)
"ST. LEO THE GREAT," BORN IN TUSCANY

If you are looking for the way by which you should go, take Christ, for he is himself the way.

ST. THOMAS AQUINAS (1225–1274)
ITALIAN DOMINICAN FRIAR, THEOLOGIAN
AND DOCTOR OF THE CHURCH

A true Christian is a man who never for a moment forgets what God has done for him in Christ, and whose whole comportment and whole activity have their root in the sentiment of gratitude.

JOHN BAILLIE (1886–1960)
SCOTTISH THEOLOGIAN AND ECUMENICAL LEADER

However one may analyse in detail the work of Christ for us and in us, one must always at last sum it up and draw it together in the simple formula: "He in us and we in him."

H. A. HODGES (1905–1976)
ENGLISH ANGLICAN THEOLOGIAN

To be like Christ is to be a Christian.

WILLIAM PENN (1644–1718)
ENGLISH QUAKER AND FOUNDER OF PENNSYLVANIA

In the middle of the night I was awakened. The room was in total darkness. Instantly sensing something alive, electric in the room, I sat bolt upright in bed. Past all credible belief, suddenly, unaccountably, Christ was there, in Person, standing by the right side of my bed.

CATHERINE MARSHALL (1914–1983)
AMERICAN RELIGIOUS WRITER

The man of prayer finds his happiness in continually creating, searching, being with Christ.

ROGER OF TAIZÉ
PRIOR OF TAIZÉ COMMUNITY IN FRANCE

The correct perspective is to see following Christ not only as the necessity it is, but as the fulfillment of the highest human possibilities and as life on the highest plane.

DALLAS WILLARD
SOUTHERN BAPTIST MINISTER, THEOLOGIAN AND SCHOLAR
THE SPIRIT OF THE DISCIPLINES:
UNDERSTANDING HOW GOD CHANGES LIVES, 1988

Conversion is a gift and an achievement. . . . While salvation cannot be attained by discipline around an unsurrendered self, nevertheless when the self is surrendered to Christ and a new center formed, then you can discipline your life around that new center—Christ. Discipline is the fruit of conversion—not the root.

E. STANLEY JONES (1884-1972)
AMERICAN MISSIONARY AND EVANGELIST
CONVERSION, 1957

Lead, kindly Light, amid the encircling gloom,
Lead thou me on!
The night is dark, and I am far from home—
Lead thou me on!
Keep thou my feet; I do not ask to see
The distant scene—one step enough for me.

JOHN HENRY NEWMAN (1801-1890)
ENGLISH CARDINAL AND LEADER OF THE OXFORD MOVEMENT
"LIGHT IN THE DARKNESS"

We get no deeper into Christ than we allow him to get into us.

JOHN HENRY JOWETT (1841-1923)
ENGLISH CONGREGATIONALIST PREACHER AND WRITER

When we have travelled all ways, we shall come to
the End of all ways, who says, *I am the way.*

ST. AMBROSE (C. 339–397)
BISHOP OF MILAN AND CHURCH FATHER
"EXPLANATION OF PSALM 118"

To know how to talk with Jesus is a great art, and to
know how to cling to him is great wisdom. Be
humble and peaceful and Jesus will be with you; be
devout and quiet and he will remain with you. You
will quickly drive him away and lose his grace,
though, if you divert your attention to
your own affairs at his expense.

THOMAS À KEMPIS (C. 1380–1471)
GERMAN MONK, MYSTIC AND WRITER
THE IMITATION OF CHRIST

At last, when truth has had its whole effect on our
minds, it will gain its fullness of authority by
becoming to us simply the echo of our own thought.
We shall find we think as Christ thought. Thus we
shall be one with him and with him
one in the Father.

RALPH WALDO EMERSON (1803–1882)
AMERICAN ESSAYIST, POET AND PHILOSOPHER
SERMON LXXVI, 1830

It is time that Christians were judged more by their likeness to Christ than their notions of Christ.

LUCRETIA MOTT (1793–1880)
QUAKER PREACHER AND SOCIAL REFORMER
SERMON ON LIKENESS TO CHRIST, 1849

There is no greater cure for hypocrisy than to live in the light of the second coming of Christ.

ANNE GRAHAM LOTZ
BIBLE TEACHER AND FOUNDER OF ANGEL MINISTRIES
THE VISION OF HIS GLORY, 1996

Make it a life-habit to copy the Lord Jesus Christ, the things he did and forbade to do, his life and passion, and think of him at all times as he did for us.

MEISTER JOHANNES ECKHART (1260–1328)
GERMAN DOMINICAN MYSTIC

Jesus Christ has true excellency, and so great an excellency, that when you come to truly see Him, you look no further, but your mind rests there.

JONATHAN EDWARDS (1703–1758)
AMERICAN THEOLOGIAN

All we want in Christ, we shall find in Christ. If we want little, we shall find little. If we want much, we shall find much; but if, in our utter helplessness, we cast our all on Christ, He will be to us the whole treasury of God.

HENRY BENJAMIN WHIPPLE (1822–1901)
AMERICAN EPISCOPAL BISHOP

God has made me a witness of Jesus. It is not my doing but God's. I cannot do other than confess him as Lord, for I know no other source of life.

LESSLIE NEWBIGIN (1909–1998)
BRITISH REFORMED THEOLOGIAN, MISSIONARY
AND ECUMENICAL LEADER

Never consent to do anything without first of all realising its significance and constructive value in Jesus Christ, and pursuing it with all your might. This is the very path to sanctity for each man according to his state and calling.

PIERRE TEILHARD DE CHARDIN (1881–1955)
FRENCH JESUIT PHILOSOPHER AND PALEONTOLOGIST
LE MILIEU DIVIN, 1957

Believing, then, is directing the heart's attention to Jesus. It is lifting the mind to "behold the lamb of God," and never ceasing that beholding for the rest of our lives.

A. W. TOZER (AIDEN WILSON TOZER) (1897–1963)
AMERICAN PASTOR AND WRITER
THE PURSUIT OF GOD, 1948

Jesus does not want you to become a Christian. He wants you to become a new creation! There is a great difference between the two.

RICHARD C. HALVERSON (1916–1995)
CHAPLAIN OF THE U.S. SENATE

❖

*B*ehold, I stand at the door, and knock; if any man hear my voice, and open the door, I will come in to him.

REVELATION 3:20 (KJV)

JESUS AS SAVIOR

For God so loved the world that he gave his one and only Son,
that whoever believes in him shall not perish but have eternal life.

JOHN 3:16

Just as I am, without one plea
But that Thy blood was shed for me,
And that Thou bidd'st me come to Thee
O Lamb of God, I come, I come!

CHARLOTTE ELLIOTT (1789–1871)
ENGLISH HYMN WRITER
HYMN, "JUST AS I AM"

In the evening I went very unwillingly to a society in
Aldersgate Street, where one was reading Luther's
preface to the epistle to the Romans. About a quarter
before nine, while he was describing the change
which God works in the heart through faith in
Christ, I felt my heart strangely warmed. I felt I did

trust in Christ, Christ alone for salvation; and an
assurance was given me that he had taken away *my*
sins, even *mine*, and saved *me* from the
law of sin and death.

JOHN WESLEY (1703-1791)
ENGLISH PREACHER AND FOUNDER OF METHODISM
JOURNAL, 24 MAY 1738
(REFERRING TO HIS CONVERSION)

This is that night of tears, that three days' space,
Sorrow abiding of the eventide,
Until the day break with the risen Christ,
And hearts that sorrowed shall be satisfied.

PETER ABELARD (1079-1142)
FRENCH PHILOSOPHER AND THEOLOGIAN
"GOOD FRIDAY: THE THIRD NOCTURNE"

Salvation happens here and now. It is always in the
present that God acts to heal and reconcile, entering
into the disruption of human lives at great cost to
himself, in order to share our predicament and
release us from it. This may seem obvious, and if we
examine the hymns of popular piety, we can often
detect just such an appeal to a present experience of
atonement, expressed in phrases like "Jesus *saves.*"
It is ironic, however, that when this devotion has
been translated into sermons it has often emerged as

more equivalent to "Jesus *saved.*" For there is a
great deal of difference between believing that God
"saves" through Christ, and believing that we
simply claim the benefits of a salvation that has
already happened, a deal that has already
been concluded.

PAUL S. FIDDES
PRINCIPAL, REGENT'S PARK COLLEGE, OXFORD UNIVERSITY
PAST EVENT AND PRESENT SALVATION:
THE CHRISTIAN IDEA OF ATONEMENT, 1989

The only article of faith, which the scripture maketh
simply necessary to salvation, is this, that
Jesus is the Christ.

THOMAS HOBBES (1588-1679)
ENGLISH POLITICAL PHILOSOPHER
LEVIATHAN, 1651

In the Gospels the Lord Jesus is presented as the
Friend of sinners, for historically he was found, first
of all, moving among the people as their Friend
before he became their Savior. But do you realize that
today He is still in the first place our Friend, in
order that He may become our Savior?

WATCHMAN NEE (NI TO-SHENG) (1903-1972)
CHINESE CHRISTIAN LEADER
(IMPRISONED BY THE COMMUNIST GOVERNMENT)

Question 31: *Why is he called "Christ," that is, the "Anointed One"?*

Because he is ordained by God the Father and anointed with the Holy Spirit to be our chief Prophet and Teacher, fully revealing to us the secret purpose and will of God concerning our redemption; to be our only High Priest, having redeemed us by the one sacrifice of his body and ever interceding for us with the Father; and to be our eternal King, governing by his Word and Spirit, and defending and sustaining us in the redemption he has won for us.

THE HEIDELBERG CATECHISM, 1562

A man who was completely innocent offered himself as a sacrifice for the good of others, including his enemies, and became the ransom of the world.
It was a perfect act.

MAHATMA GANDHI (MOHANDAS KARAMCHAND GANDHI)
(1869-1948)
INDIAN STATESMAN AND PACIFIST
NON-VIOLENCE IN PEACE AND WAR, 1949
(REFERRING TO JESUS)

Once saved, always saved.

AUTHOR UNKNOWN
MOTTO OF THE REFORMATION

The blood of Jesus can cover a multitude of sins,
it seems to me.

DENIS DIDEROT (1713-1784)
FRENCH PHILOSOPHER AND MAN OF LETTERS

I call consolation any increase of faith, hope, and
charity and any interior joy that calls and attracts to
heavenly things, and to the salvation of one's soul,
inspiring it with peace and quiet in Christ our Lord.

ST. IGNATIUS OF LOYOLA (1491-1556)
BASQUE MYSTIC AND FOUNDER OF THE JESUIT ORDER
THE SPIRITUAL EXERCISES

Man of Sorrows! what a name
For the Son of God, who came
Ruined sinners to reclaim!
Hallelujah, what a Savior!

PHILIP PAUL BLISS (1838-1876)
AMERICAN EVANGELIST
HYMN, "MAN OF SORROWS! WHAT A NAME"

Christianity is a rescue religion. It declares that God
has taken the initiative in Jesus Christ to deliver us
from our sins. This is the main theme of the Bible.

JOHN R. W. STOTT
RECTOR EMERITUS OF ALL SOULS CHURCH, LONDON
BASIC CHRISTIANITY, 1958

Christ came to save all through his own person.

ST. IRENAEUS (C. 130-202)
BISHOP OF LYONS

Lord Jesus Christ, Son of God, have mercy on me,
a sinner.

"THE JESUS PRAYER" (ELEVENTH CENTURY)

When I read that Christ Jesus came into the world
to save sinners, it was as if day suddenly
broke on a dark night.

THOMAS BILNEY (SIXTEENTH CENTURY)
ENGLISH PROTESTANT MARTYR

You have trusted Christ as your dying savior; now
trust Him as your living savior. Just as much as he
came to deliver you from future punishment, did he
also come to deliver you from present bondage.

HANNAH WHITALL SMITH (1832-1911)
QUAKER EVANGELIST

The God of the resurrection is awake
all the time. . . .

GEORGE MACDONALD (1824-1905)
SCOTTISH NOVELIST, POET AND PASTOR
"THE RESURRECTION HARVEST"

To know Christ is not to speculate about the mode of his incarnation, but to know his saving benefits.

PHILIP MELANCHTHON (1497-1560)
LUTHERAN THEOLOGIAN

The Church's one foundation
Is Jesus Christ her Lord:
She is His new creation
By water and the word;
From heaven he came and sought her
To be His holy bride:
With His own blood he bought her,
And for her life He died.

SAMUEL JOHN STONE (1839-1900)
ENGLISH CLERGYMAN
HYMN, "THE CHURCH'S ONE FOUNDATION," 1866

Christ came to earth for one reason: to give his life as a ransom for you, for me, for all of us. He sacrificed himself to give us a second chance. He would have gone to any lengths to do so. And he did. He went to the cross, where man's utter despair collided with God's unbending grace.

MAX LUCADO
AMERICAN PASTOR AND AUTHOR
THE GIFT FOR ALL PEOPLE, 1999

The creative Charity of God, as experienced by man, is a redemptive force. It comes into human life in Christ, his Spirit, his Church, his sacraments, and his saints, not to inform but to transform; to rescue from the downward pull which is felt throughout the natural order, to reform, energize, and at last sanctify the souls of men, making those rescued souls in turn part of the redeeming organism through which the salvation of the world will be achieved.

EVELYN UNDERHILL (1875–1941)
ENGLISH MYSTICAL WRITER

O Lamb of God, who takest away the sin of the world, look upon us and have mercy upon us; thou who art thyself both Victim and Priest, thyself both Reward and Redeemer, keep us safe from all evil those whom thou hast redeemed,
O Savior of the world.

ST. IRENAEUS (c. 130–202)
BISHOP OF LYONS

Christ is not said to have received salvation, but to be salvation itself.

JOHN CALVIN (1509–1564)
FRENCH-BORN REFORMATION THEOLOGIAN

Just as a grain of wheat must die in the earth in order to bring forth a rich harvest, so your Son died on the cross to bring a rich harvest of love. Just as the harvest of wheat must be ground into flour to make bread, so the suffering of your Son brings us the bread of life. Just as bread gives our bodies strength for our daily work, so the risen body of your Son gives us strength to obey your laws.

THOMAS MUNZER (C. 1490-1525)
GERMAN ANABAPTIST AND REFORMER

Christ the Lord is risen today, Alleluia!
Sons of men and angels say, Alleluia!
Raise your joys and triumphs high, Alleluia!
Sing, ye heavens, and earth, reply, Alleluia!

CHARLES WESLEY (1707-1788)
ENGLISH METHODIST PREACHER AND HYMN WRITER
HYMN, "CHRIST THE LORD IS RISEN TODAY," 1737

Conquering kings their titles take
From the foes they captive make;
Jesu, by a nobler deed
From the thousands He hath freed.

JOHN CHANDLER (1806-1876)
ENGLISH CLERGYMAN
HYMN, "CONQUERING KINGS THEIR TITLES TAKE"

Jesus did not come merely to disclose God's character. He came to make it possible to be remade in the likeness of that character. He came to redeem us from what we are and to remake us in the likeness of what he is. He is not merely a teacher, a doer—he is a redeemer.

E. STANLEY JONES (1884-1972)
AMERICAN METHODIST MISSIONARY AND EVANGELIST
A SONG OF ASCENTS, 1968

The Gospel of Jesus Christ is news, good news: the best and most important news any human being ever hears.
The Gospel declares the only way to know God in peace, love, and joy is through the reconciling death of Christ the risen Lord.

THE COMMITTEE ON EVANGELICAL UNITY
IN THE GOSPEL
THIS WE BELIEVE: THE GOSPEL OF JESUS CHRIST-
AN EVANGELICAL CELEBRATION, 2000

Eighty-six years have I served Christ, and He has never done me wrong. How can I blaspheme my King who saved me?

POLYCARP (C. 69-155)
BISHOP OF SMYRNA
(BURNED AT THE STAKE FOR REFUSING
TO WORSHIP CAESAR AS A GOD)

To know about Christ is not enough. To be convinced that He is the Savior of the world is not enough. To affirm our faith in Him, as we do in the Apostles' Creed, is not enough. To believe that He has saved others is not enough. We really don't actively believe in Christ until we make a commitment of our lives to Him and receive Him as our Savior.

BILLY GRAHAM (WILLIAM FRANKLIN GRAHAM JR.)
AMERICAN EVANGELICAL LEADER AND WRITER
THE SECRET OF HAPPINESS, 1955

You may study, look, and meditate, but Jesus is a greater Savior than you think Him to be, even when your thoughts are at their highest.

CHARLES HADDON SPURGEON (1834–1892)
ENGLISH NONCONFORMIST PREACHER
"NO GREATER SAVIOR"

Neither the kingdoms of this world nor the bounds of the universe have any use for me. I would rather die for Jesus Christ than rule the last reaches of the earth. My search is for Him Who died for us; my love is for Him Who rose for our salvation.

ST. IGNATIUS OF ANTIOCH (C. SECOND CENTURY)
BISHOP OF ANTIOCH IN SYRIA
(ON THE LETTER TO THE ROMANS)

For if it be true that one dead can exert no power,
while the Saviour does daily so many works, drawing
men to religion, persuading to virtue, teaching of
immortality, leading on to a desire for heavenly
things, revealing the knowledge of the Father,
inspiring strength to meet death, showing himself to
each one, and displacing the godlessness of idolatry,
and the gods and spirits of the unbelievers can do
none of these things . . . whereas by the sign of the
cross all magic is stopped, and all witchcraft brought
to naught, and all the idols are being deserted and
left, and every unruly pleasure is checked, and every
one is looking up from earth to heaven—whom
is one to pronounce dead?

ST. ATHANASIUS (296–373)
BISHOP OF ALEXANDRIA
(ON THE INCARNATION OF THE WORD)

He entered this world, took on human flesh, and
died on a cross to bear your sin, to pay the penalty
for your iniquity, to remove your guilt. He did it so
that you might enter into his presence.
You must respond.

JOHN MACARTHUR
AMERICAN THEOLOGIAN AND PASTOR

The action of Christ who is risen on mankind whom
he redeemed fails not, but increases.

LORD ACTON (1834-1902)
BRITISH HISTORIAN

The Son of glory came down, and was slain,
Us whom he had made, and Satan stole, to unbind.
'Twas much, that man was made like God before,
But, that God should be made like man, much more.

JOHN DONNE (1572-1631)
ENGLISH POET AND DIVINE
"HOLY SONNET XV"

There is nothing that is more dangerous to your own
salvation, more unworthy of God and more harmful
to your own happiness, than that you should be
content to remain as you are.

FRANÇOIS FÉNELON (1651-1715)
FRENCH ARCHBISHOP

Keep watch in your heart; and with watchfulness say
in your mind with awe and trembling: "Lord Jesus
Christ, have mercy upon me."

PHILIMON (C. SIXTH CENTURY)
EGYPTIAN MONK

If the key is prayer, the door is Jesus Christ. How good of God to provide us a way into his heart. He knows that we are stiff-necked and hard-hearted, so he has provided a means of entrance. Jesus, the Christ, lived a perfect life, died in our place, and rose victorious over all the dark powers so that we might live through him.

RICHARD J. FOSTER
QUAKER THEOLOGIAN, WRITER AND
PROFESSOR OF SPIRITUAL FORMATION
PRAYER: FINDING THE HEART'S TRUE HOME, 1992

We do not presume to come to this thy table, O merciful Lord, trusting in our own righteousness, but in thy manifold and great mercies; we be not worthy so much as to gather up the crumbs under the table. But thou are the same Lord, whose property is always to have mercy: Grant us therefore gracious Lord so to eat the flesh of thy dear son Jesus, and so to drink his blood in these holy mysteries, that we may continually dwell in him, and he in us, that our sinful bodies may be made clean by his body, and our souls washed through his most precious blood. Amen.

THE ORDER OF COMMUNION
ENGLISH SUPPLEMENT TO THE LATIN PRAYER BOOK, 1548

I must tell Jesus all of my trials;
I cannot bear this burden alone.
In my distress He kindly will help me;
He ever loves and cares for His own. . . .

Tempted and tried, I need a great Saviour,
One who can help my burdens to bear.
I must tell Jesus, I must tell Jesus;
He all my cares and sorrows will share.

ELISHA A. HOFFMAN (1839-1929)
AMERICAN MINISTER AND GOSPEL HYMN WRITER
HYMN, "I MUST TELL JESUS"

The blood is the poured-out life of the Son of God,
given as the price, the atonement, the substitute, for
the forfeited life of the believer in Jesus Christ. Any
sinner who receives Christ as God's gift is
cleansed from all sin by his blood.

MARCUS RAINSFORD (NINETEENTH CENTURY)
IRISH PREACHER AND EVANGELIST

Faith in a risen Saviour is necessary if the vague
stirrings toward immortality are to bring us to restful
and satisfying communion with God.

A. W. TOZER (AIDEN WILSON TOZER) (1897-1963)
AMERICAN PASTOR AND WRITER
THE PURSUIT OF GOD, 1948

The New Testament never simply says "remember Jesus Christ." That is a half-finished sentence. It says "remember Jesus Christ is risen from the dead."

ROBERT RUNCIE
ENGLISH ARCHBISHOP OF CANTERBURY
SEASONS OF THE SPIRIT, 1983

God rest you merry, gentlemen,
Let nothing you dismay,
For Jesus Christ, our Saviour,
Was born upon this day,
To save us all from Satan's power
When we were gone astray.
O tidings of comfort and joy!
For Jesus Christ, our Saviour,
Was born on Christmas Day.

DINAH MARIA MULOCK CRAIK (1826–1887)
BRITISH POET
CHRISTMAS CAROL, "GOD REST YOU MERRY, GENTLEMEN"

In the Cross, God descends to bear in his own heart the sins of the world. In Jesus, he atones at unimaginable cost to himself.

WOODROW A. GEIER
RELIGION IN LIFE, 1947

Crown Him with many crowns,
The Lamb upon His throne;
Hark! how the heavenly anthem drowns
All music but its own.
Awake my soul, and sing
Of Him who died for thee;
And hail Him as thy matchless King
Through all eternity.

MATTHEW BRIDGES (1800-1894)
HYMN, "CROWN HIM WITH MANY CROWNS," 1851

It happened to me as it happens to a man who goes out on some business, and on the way suddenly decides that the business is unnecessary, and returns home. The direction of my life and my desires became different, and good and evil changed places. . . . I, like the thief on the Cross, have believed in Christ's teaching and been saved.

LEO TOLSTOY (1828-1910)
RUSSIAN NOVELIST

All my theology is reduced to this narrow compass—Jesus Christ came into the world to save sinners.

ARCHIBALD ALEXANDER (1772-1851)
AMERICAN PRESBYTERIAN PROFESSOR AT PRINCETON
THEOLOGICAL SEMINARY

*B*ehold the Lamb of God, which taketh away the sin of the world.

JOHN 1:29 (KJV)

THE POWER OF
THE CROSS

*T*hen Jesus said to his disciples, "If anyone would come after me, he must deny himself and take up his cross and follow me. For whoever wants to save his life will lose it, but whoever loses his life for me will find it."

MATTHEW 16:24-25

The Son of God was crucified . . . died . . . was buried and rose again. The fact is certain, because it is impossible.

TERTULLIAN (C. 160-225)
CHURCH FATHER FROM CARTHAGE

Onward, Christian soldiers,
Marching as to war,

*With the Cross of Jesus
Going on before.*

SABINE BARING-GOULD (1834–1924)
ENGLISH CLERGYMAN
HYMN, "ONWARD, CHRISTIAN SOLDIERS," 1864

No pain, no palm; no thorns, no throne; no gall,
no glory; no cross, no crown.

WILLIAM PENN (1644–1718)
ENGLISH QUAKER AND FOUNDER OF PENNSYLVANIA
PAMPHLET, 1669

The cross is central. It is struck into the middle of
the world, into the middle of time, into the middle of
destiny. The cross is struck into the heart of God.

FREDERICK W. NORWOOD
PASTOR OF THE CITY TEMPLE, LONDON
"TODAY IS MINE"

Like Buddha under the Bo tree, Jesus, on his tree,
has his eyes closed too. The difference is this. The
pain and sadness of the world that Buddha's eyes
close out is the pain and sadness of the world
that the eyes of Jesus close in.

FREDERICK BUECHNER
AMERICAN AWARD-WINNING AUTHOR AND APOLOGIST

The tree is for me a plant of eternal salvation. By it I am nourished, by it I am fed. By its roots I am firmly planted. By its branches, I am spread out, its perfume is a delight to me, and its spirit refreshes me like a delightful wind. . . . By its peak which touches the height of the heavens, by its base which supports the earth, and by its immense arms subduing the many spirits of the air on every side, it exists in its totality in every thing and in every place.

PSEUDO-HIPPOLYTUS (C. THIRD CENTURY)
ANONYMOUS PASCHALE HOMILY

The death of Jesus on the cross is the *centre* of all Christian theology. It is not the only theme of theology, but it is in effect the entry to its problems and answer on earth. All Christian statements about God, about creation, about sin and death have their focal point in the crucified Christ. All Christian statements about history, about the church, about faith and sanctification, about the future and about hope stem from the crucified Christ.

JÜRGEN MOLTMANN
GERMAN PROFESSOR OF SYSTEMATIC THEOLOGY
THE CRUCIFIED GOD, 1973

Be an example to all of denying yourself and
taking up your cross daily.

JOHN WESLEY (1703-1791)
ENGLISH PREACHER AND FOUNDER OF METHODISM
A PLAIN ACCOUNT OF CHRISTIAN PERFECTION

The only way of winning a knowledge of the Cross is
by feeling the whole weight of the Cross.

EDITH STEIN (1891-1942)
GERMAN CARMELITE NUN
(DIED IN AUSCHWITZ)

*The cross is the way of the lost
the cross is the staff of the lame
the cross is the guide of the blind
the cross is the strength of the weak
the cross is the hope of the hopeless
the cross is the freedom of the slaves
the cross is the water of the seeds
the cross is the consolation of the labourers
the cross is the source of those who seek water
the cross is the cloth of the naked.*

AFRICAN HYMN (TENTH CENTURY)
QUOTED IN *THE DOUBLEDAY CHRISTIAN QUOTATION
COLLECTION*, 1998

The story of Christ crucified was kept alive by word of mouth in the early Christian churches and homes. It was not until the fifth and sixth centuries that the first crucifix appeared, and then, for a very long time, the figure of Christ on it was not Christ crucified but Christ risen from the dead.

P. J. SMITH
QUOTED IN *THE JESUS BOOK*, 1978

Crucified inwardly and outwardly with Christ, you will live in this life with fullness and satisfaction of soul, and possess your soul in patience.

ST. JOHN OF THE CROSS (1542–1591)
SPANISH CARMELITE PRIEST AND MYSTIC

If we would view every object in its true light, and rightly estimate its nature and design, we must consider it with reference to Christ and his cross. To the cross of Christ all eternity has looked forward: to the cross of Christ all eternity will look back.

EDWARD PAYSON (1783–1827)
AMERICAN CONGREGATIONALIST PASTOR AND PREACHER

A cross is not just a piece of wood. It is everything
that makes life difficult.

LEONARDO BOFF
BRAZILIAN LIBERATION THEOLOGIAN

The cross is the central symbol of Christianity. Many
cathedrals have been built in the shape of the cross.
Their towers are crowned with the symbol. Every
mass is a reenactment of the sacrificial death of
Christ. One can hardly turn in any direction without
seeing a cross on a hill, on a church, or as a piece of
jewelry. This universal symbol is understood by
virtually everyone. Its very sight calls to mind
Christ's first-century execution. It is his
salvation symbol.

CALVIN MILLER
AMERICAN BAPTIST PROFESSOR AND PASTOR
THE BOOK OF JESUS, 1996

Those holy fields
Over whose acres walk'd those blessed feet
Which, fourteen hundred years ago, were nail'd
For our advantage on the bitter cross.

WILLIAM SHAKESPEARE (1564–1616)
ENGLISH DRAMATIST
PLAY, *HENRY IV*

The strong hands of God twisted the crown of
thorns into a crown of glory: and in such hands
we are safe.

CHARLES WILLIAMS (1889-1945)
ENGLISH THEOLOGIAN AND POET

The cross of Christ is the Jacob's ladder by which
we ascend into the highest heaven.

THOMAS TRAHERNE (C. 1636-1674)
ENGLISH ANGLICAN POET AND WRITER

There is a green hill far away,
Without a city wall,
Where the dear Lord was crucified,
Who died to save us all.

CECIL FRANCES ALEXANDER (1818-1895)
IRISH HYMN WRITER
HYMN, "THERE IS A GREEN HILL"

Cheap grace is grace without discipleship, grace
without the cross, grace without Jesus Christ,
living and incarnate.

DIETRICH BONHOEFFER (1905-1945)
GERMAN LUTHERAN PASTOR AND THEOLOGIAN
(IMPRISONED AND EXECUTED BY THE NAZIS)

In this sign shalt thou conquer.
(*In Hoc Signo Vinces*)

CONSTANTINE THE GREAT (C. 288-337)
ROMAN EMPEROR FROM 306
(THESE WORDS AND THE SIGN OF THE CROSS
WERE SAID TO HAVE APPEARED IN THE SKY
TO CONSTANTINE AND HIS SOLDIERS)

The story of the cross—the terrible story of one who
is falsely accused, abandoned by his friends, stripped
and humiliated, who cries out in pain, who
experiences desolation and loss, who dies a ghastly
death, parched and thirsty—is also the beautiful story
of the God who comes to earth to share our
humanity, who dies to share our dying, and who rises
again to show us death is not the end and to create a
new communion between earth and heaven.

STEPHEN COTTRELL
CANON PASTOR OF PETERBOROUGH CATHEDRAL
I THIRST, 2003

Jesus was crucified, not in a cathedral between two
candles, but on a cross between two thieves.

GEORGE F. MACLEOD (1895-1991)
SCOTTISH PRESBYTERIAN MINISTER

The Cross is God at work.

PAUL CLAUDEL (1868-1955)
FRENCH POET AND WRITER

To remember Jesus is to remember
first of all his Cross.

JOHN KNOX (1505-1572)
SCOTTISH PROTESTANT REFORMER
THE CHURCH AND THE REALITY OF CHRIST

Nothing in my hand I bring,
Simply to Thy Cross I cling.

AUGUSTUS MONTAGUE TOPLADY (1740-1778)
ENGLISH CLERGYMAN
HYMN, "ROCK OF AGES"

The Way of the Cross winds through our towns and
cities, our hospitals and factories, and through our
battlefields; it takes the road of poverty and
suffering in every form.
It is in front of these new Stations of the Cross that
we must stop and meditate and pray to the suffering
Christ for strength to love him enough to act.

MICHAEL QUOIST
FRENCH CATHOLIC PRIEST AND POET
PRAYERS OF LIFE, 1963

The cross of Christ declares two things: first,
God's infinite love of the world; second,
God's infinite hatred of sin.

R. A. TORREY (REUBEN ARCHER TORREY) (1856–1928)
AMERICAN EVANGELIST, EDUCATOR AND WRITER

There is a whole range of ways in which we can
begin to comprehend the objective, creative power of
the cross of Jesus. . . . Above all, a doctrine of God
which takes his suffering seriously will link our
present experience of God to the past
event of the cross.

PAUL S. FIDDES
PRINCIPAL, REGENT'S PARK COLLEGE, OXFORD UNIVERSITY
*PAST EVENT AND PRESENT SALVATION:
THE CHRISTIAN IDEA OF ATONEMENT*, 1989

When Jesus died that appallingly harrowing death,
his life seemed to have terminated in complete
failure and disaster. The world's opinion of the
event, instead, proved to be strangely different,
providing the greatest paradox in all history.

MICHAEL GRANT
PRESIDENT OF THE CLASSICAL ASSOCIATION OF ENGLAND
JESUS, 1977

When the love of God is poured out to us through the cross of Christ, it empowers us to do remarkable things in God's name.

MICHAEL DUBRUIEL
AMERICAN CATHOLIC WRITER
THE POWER OF THE CROSS, 2004

The single, overwhelming fact of history is the crucifixion of Jesus Christ. There is no military battle, no geographical exploration, no scientific discovery, no literary creation, no artistic achievement, no moral heroism that compares with it. It is unique, massive, monumental, unprecedented, and unparalleled. . . . The cross of Christ is the central fact to which all other facts are subordinate.

EUGENE H. PETERSON
AMERICAN PRESBYTERIAN CHURCH PASTOR AND WRITER

Christ's suffering on the cross is the focal point of the Christian faith. That's where His deity, humanity, work, and suffering are most clearly seen.

JOHN MACARTHUR
AMERICAN THEOLOGIAN AND PASTOR
TRUTH FOR TODAY, 2001

Lord, by this sweet and saving sign,
Defend us from our foes and thine.
Jesus, by thy wounded feet,
Direct our path aright:
Jesus, by thy nailed hands,
Move ours to deeds of love:
Jesus, by thy pierced side,
Cleanse our desires:
Jesus, by thy crown of thorns,
Annihilate our pride:
Jesus, by thy silence,
Shame our complaints:
Jesus, by thy parched lips,
Curb our cruel speech:
Jesus, by thy closing eyes,
Look on our sin no more:
Jesus, by thy broken heart,
Knit ours to thee.
And by this sweet and saving sign,
Lord, draw us to our peace and thine.

RICHARD CRASHAW (C. 1612-1649) AND OTHERS
ENGLISH POET
FROM *A TIME TO PRAY*, 1998

What Jesus suffered then for us and for our salvation
we cannot know, for during those three hours he
hung upon his cross in silence and darkness. . . . But
towards the close of that time his anguish culminated
and, drinking to the very deepest dregs the cup of
humiliation and bitterness, he uttered that mysterious
cry, the full significance of which will never be
fathomed by man—"ELI, ELI, LAMA
SABACHTHANI?", "My God, my God,
why hast thou forsaken me?"

F. W. FARRAR (1831–1903)
CHAPLAIN TO THE QUEEN AND CANON OF WESTMINSTER
THE LIFE OF CHRIST, 1874

The resurrection means that he can bring forth the
new. His working never comes to an end, for he can
always open up a new possibility. . . . The cross
speaks of God standing with his creatures in the flux
of events; the resurrection speaks of his always being
ahead of events. Both symbols seem essential
to the idea of God.

JOHN MACQUARRIE
SCOTTISH THEOLOGIAN
PRINCIPLES OF CHRISTIAN THEOLOGY, 1977

The cross is the supreme evidence of
the love of God.

ERICH SAUER
THE TRIUMPH OF THE CRUCIFIED, 1957

When I survey the wondrous cross,
On which the Prince of Glory died,
My richest gain I count but loss,
And pour contempt on all my pride. . . .

Were the whole realm of nature mine,
That were a present far too small;
Love so amazing, so divine,
Demands my soul, my life, my all.

ISAAC WATTS (1674–1748)
ENGLISH HYMN WRITER
HYMN, "CRUCIFIXION TO THE WORLD,
BY THE CROSS OF CHRIST," 1707
(ALSO KNOWN AS "WHEN I SURVEY THE WONDROUS CROSS")

The cross of Christ, which is granted for the
salvation of mortals, is both a mystery and an
example: a mystery by which the power of God is
shown forth; an example, by which man's
devotion is aroused.

POPE LEO I (FIFTH CENTURY)
"ST. LEO THE GREAT," BORN IN TUSCANY

Doing what Jesus did in all situations will make you a better person here on earth. Accepting what Jesus did on the cross will secure your eternal future. Why not do both? The decision is yours.

BRUCE BICKEL AND STAN JANTZ
GOD IS IN THE SMALL STUFF–AND IT ALL MATTERS, 1998

The Christianity of the future has to face not simply philosophical questions, but a moral critique and a continuing question mark about how it can convey a message of hope that does not seem a cheap evasion of the continuing human tragedy. Its hope must be that it lives, and can only live, in the power of the crucified one.

RICHARD HARRIES
ENGLISH ANGLICAN BISHOP OF OXFORD
CHRISTIANITY: TWO THOUSAND YEARS, 2001

The cross.
It rests on the time line of history like a compelling diamond. Its tragedy summons all sufferers. Its absurdity attracts all cynics. Its hope lures all searchers.

MAX LUCADO
AMERICAN PASTOR AND AUTHOR
NO WONDER THEY CALL HIM THE SAVIOR, 1986

If you would understand that the cross is Christ's triumph, hear what he himself said: "I, if I am lifted up, will draw all people to myself." See now that the cross is Christ's glory and triumph.

ANDREW OF CRETE (660–740)
DAMASCAN HYMN WRITER

If you rightly bear your cross, it will bear you.

THOMAS À KEMPIS (C. 1380–1471)
GERMAN MONK, MYSTIC AND WRITER
THE IMITATION OF CHRIST

Every sin and every sorrow,
Every ill that life can borrow,
In the Cross will gain surcease;
In the Cross, though sore and grieving,
He that humbly seeks relieving,
Findeth refuge, findeth peace.

ST. BONAVENTURE (1221–1274)
TUSCAN-BORN FRANCISCAN THEOLOGIAN
"RECORDARE SANCTAE CRUCIS"

The world is my crucifix.
(*Mundus mihi crucifixus est.*)

MEDIEVAL MOTTO OF THE CARTHUSIAN ORDER

The world is full of mysteries; the soul is full of mysteries; heaven is all mystery to us earthly creatures. But whoever embraces the cross with open heart finds therein the explanation of a thousand mysteries.

WILLIAM BERNARD ULLATHORNE (1806–1889)
ENGLISH BENEDICTINE MONK AND BISHOP
"HUMILITY AND PATIENCE"

To know Jesus and Him crucified is my philosophy, and there is none higher.

ST. BERNARD OF CLAIRVAUX (1091–1153)
FRENCH MONK AND FOUNDER OF THE CISTERCIAN ORDER
COMMENTARY ON THE CANTICLE OF CANTICLES

Behold the Man! Who wore
A crown of thorns for me:
And in His sacred person bore
Our sins upon the tree:
Our sins upon the tree,
Thus full honor made,
Through Him whose love beyond degree
Our ransom paid.

MATTHEW BRIDGES (1800–1894)
HYMN, "ECCE HOMO"

Easter is the interpretation of Good Friday. The significance of the Cross is revealed in the Resurrection. The Resurrection is not so much a mere sequel to the Cross; or a reversal of the Cross; or a subsequent reward because of the endurance of the Cross. Rather, it is a revealing of what the Cross already was.

R. C. MOBERLY (1845–1903)
ENGLISH THEOLOGIAN AND OXFORD DIVINE
"CHRIST OUR LIFE"

The cross of poverty, the cross of hunger, the cross of every other sort of suffering can be transformed since Christ's Cross has become a light in our world. It is a light of hope and salvation. It gives meaning to all human suffering. It brings with it the promise of an eternal life, free from sorrow, free from sin.

POPE JOHN PAUL II (1920–2005)
POLISH PRIEST AND PHILOSOPHER
AGENDA FOR THE THIRD MILLENNIUM, 1996

The way of the Cross is the way of light.
(*Via Crucis, Via Lucis*)

MEDIEVAL LATIN PROVERB

He is the Vine, because He spread out the branches
of His arms that the world might pluck in clusters
the grapes of consolation from the cross.

NICETA OF REMESIANA (C. 335–414)
DACIAN BISHOP

O Christ, give us patience, and a faith and hope as
we kneel at the foot of Thy cross and hold fast to it.
Teach us by Thy cross that however ill the world
may go, the Father so loved us that
he spared not Thee.

CHARLES KINGSLEY (1819–1875)
ENGLISH WRITER AND CLERGYMAN

In its highest and most general sense, the doctrine of
the Cross is that to which all men adhere who
believe that the vast movement and agitations of
human life open on to a road which leads
somewhere, and that that road climbs upward.

PIERRE TEILHARD DE CHARDIN (1881–1955)
FRENCH JESUIT PHILOSOPHER AND PALEONTOLOGIST
LE MILIEU DIVIN, 1957

The whole world in comparison with the cross of Christ is one grand impertinence.

ROBERT LEIGHTON (1611–1684)
SCOTTISH PRELATE AND CLASSICAL SCHOLAR

Although he died on the cross in weakness, he now lives by the mighty power of God.

2 CORINTHIANS 13:4 (NLT)

IMAGES OF JESUS

For unto us a child is born, unto us a son is given: and the government shall be upon his shoulder: and his name shall be called Wonderful, Counsellor, The mighty God, The everlasting Father, The Prince of Peace.

ISAIAH 9:6 (KJV)

Christ is given so many names because of his
limitless greatness and the treasury of his very rich
perfections and with them the host of functions and
other benefits which are born in him and spread
over us. Just as they cannot be embraced by the
soul's vision, so much less can a
single word name them.

LUIS DE LEON (C. 1527–1591)
AUGUSTINIAN CANON AND THEOLOGIAN

It is certain for us that Jesus, our Lord, is God, Son of God and King, prince, light of light, creator and counsellor and leader and way and redeemer and shepherd and gatherer and gate and pearl and lamp; and with many names he is named. But we shall now leave all these on one side, and prove that he is Son of God, and that he is God, who has come from God.

APHRAHAT THE PERSIAN SAGE (FOURTH CENTURY)
CHURCH FATHER AND MONK
"PROOFS"

The most perfect being who has ever trod the soil of this planet was called the Man of Sorrows.

JAMES ANTHONY FROUDE (1818-1894)
ENGLISH HISTORIAN AND RECTOR
OF ST. ANDREW'S UNIVERSITY

Little Jesus, wast Thou shy
Once, and just so small as I?
And what did it feel like to be
Out of heaven, and just like me?

FRANCIS THOMPSON (1859-1907)
ENGLISH POET
"EX ORE INFANTIUM"

"Christ"—as you hear this do not heed the
simplicity of the word or the brevity of the
expression. Rather, join with me in thinking of the
glory of the Godhead, which is beyond thought and
understanding. Think of God's unutterable power,
his immeasurable mercy, his inconceivable riches,
which he generously and bountifully gives to men.

ST. SYMEON THE NEW THEOLOGIAN (949-1022)
ABBOT IN CONSTANTINOPLE AND HERMIT IN ASIA MINOR
"DISCOURSES"

It does not matter whether the Christ who fills our
vision is the historical Jesus, or the living Saviour, or
the Christ of the Body and the Blood, or the Logos
and Lord of the universe, or the master and meaning
of history, or the Christ in my neighbour and in his
poor. These are only aspects of his being. In
whatever aspect he is most real to us, what
matters is that we adore him.

JOHN V. TAYLOR
ANGLICAN BISHOP OF WINCHESTER
THE GO-BETWEEN GOD, 1972

In all this diversity, as the feminist Christ, the black Christ, the poor Christ, the Pentecostal Christ, the evangelical Christ vie with older representations in a seething mix which is almost impossible to map, one other development has emerged which may well be the most significant of them all. . . . Jesus the Jew has begun to reappear from under centuries of disguise. The executed healer and preacher with whom this whole tale began has looked at us again with Jewish eyes, demanding that we take account of him.

OXFORD READERS: JESUS, 2002
DAVID F. FORD AND MIKE HIGTON, EDS.

He wanted us to believe in his goodness and to look upon him as guardian, father, teacher, adviser, and physician, as our mind, light, honour, glory, strength, and life.

AUTHOR UNKNOWN (SECOND OR THIRD CENTURY)
EPISTLE TO DIOGNETUS

In these days there appeared, and there still is, a man of great power named Jesus Christ, who is called by the Gentiles the prophet of truth, whom his disciples call the Son of God, raising the dead and healing diseases—a man in stature middling tall, and comely,

having a reverend countenance, which those who
look upon may love and fear . . . having an
expression simple and mature, the eyes grey,
flashing, and clear; in rebuke terrible, in admonition
kind and loveable, cheerful yet keeping gravity;
sometimes he has wept, but never laughed; in stature
of body tall and straight, with hands and arms fair to
look upon, in talk grave, reserved and modest,
fairer than the children of men.

AUTHOR UNKNOWN
"THE LETTER OF LENTULUS"
(ANONYMOUS LETTER, PROBABLY THIRTEENTH CENTURY
IN ORIGIN, ONCE THOUGHT TO HAVE BEEN WRITTEN
BY A ROMAN OFFICIAL IN PALESTINE AT
THE TIME OF CHRIST'S MINISTRY)

Take, then, your paltry Christ,
Your gentleman God.
We want the carpenter's son,
With his saw and hod.

FRANCIS ADAMS (1862–1893)
ENGLISH WRITER AND POET

Christ is the dazzling bright sun who covered
himself with a cloud in order to be seen.

ANTONY OF PADUA (1195–1231)
FRANCISCAN FRIAR AND PREACHER
"TO SEE THE FACE OF CHRIST"

Christ is not something added to the world as an extra, he is not an embellishment, a king as we now crown kings, the owner of a great estate. . . . He is the alpha and the omega, the principle and the end, the foundation stone and the keystone, the plenitude and the plenifier. He is the one who consummates all things and gives them their consistence.

PIERRE TEILHARD DE CHARDIN (1881-1955)
FRENCH JESUIT PHILOSOPHER AND PALEONTOLOGIST
SCIENCE AND CHRIST, 1921

Whether you think Jesus was God or not, you must admit he was a first-rate political economist.

GEORGE BERNARD SHAW (1856-1950)
IRISH DRAMATIST
PLAY, *ANDROCLES AND THE LION*

*Jesus Christ is the Completer
of unfinished people
with unfinished work
in unfinished times.*

LONA FOWLER
AMERICAN POET
"MIDDLE TIME"

> In the juvescence of the year
> came Christ the tiger.

T. S. ELIOT (THOMAS STEARNS ELIOT) (1888-1965)
ANGLO-AMERICAN POET, CRITIC AND DRAMATIST
"GERONTION"

Christian artists confronted one great problem. They
had to make clear that when representing an
historical event—the life and death of Jesus—they were
not just offering a record of the past but a continuing
truth; we the spectators have to become eye-
witnesses to an event that matters to us now.
Theological concepts must be given human
dimensions and if only words can tackle the abstract
mysteries, paintings are uniquely able to address the
universal questions through the intelligence
of the heart.

In the hand of the great artists, the different
moments and aspects of Christ's life become
archetypes of all human experience.

NEIL MACGREGOR
DIRECTOR OF THE NATIONAL GALLERY IN LONDON
"THE IMAGE OF CHRIST,"
CATALOGUE FOR THE 2000 EXHIBITION

Welcome, all wonders in one sight!
Eternity shut in a span.
Summer in winter. Day in night.
Heaven in earth, and God in Man.
Great little One! whose all-embracing birth
Lifts earth to heaven, and stoops heaven to earth.

RICHARD CRASHAW (C. 1612–1649)
ENGLISH POET
HYMN, "THE HOLY NATIVITY OF OUR LORD"

Rock of Ages, cleft for me,
Let me hide myself in thee.

AUGUSTUS MONTAGUE TOPLADY (1740–1778)
ENGLISH CLERGYMAN
HYMN, "ROCK OF AGES"

Christ is the best husband.

ST. AUGUSTINE OF HIPPO (354–430)
DOCTOR OF THE CHURCH AND PHILOSOPHER

The name of Jesus is in my mind as joyful as a song,
in my ear a heavenly music, and in my mouth
sweet honey.

RICHARD ROLLE (1290–1349)
ENGLISH SPIRITUAL WRITER AND MYSTIC

To the artist he is the one altogether lovely.
To the educator he is the master teacher.
To the philosopher he is the wisdom of God.
To the lonely he is a brother; to the sorrowful,
a comforter;
to the bereaved, the resurrection and the life.
And to the sinner he is the Lamb of God
who takes away the sin of the world.

JOHN H. GERSTNER (1914-1996)
AMERICAN PRESBYTERIAN PASTOR AND TEACHER

He is the way, because he leads us through himself;
the door, as letting us in; the shepherd, as making us
dwell in a place of green pastures, and bringing us
up by waters of rest, and leading us there, and
protecting us from wild beasts, converting the erring,
bringing back that which was lost, binding up that
which was broken, guarding the strong, and bringing
them together in the fold beyond, with words
of pastoral knowledge.

ST. GREGORY OF NAZIANZUS (c. 330-390)
CAPPADOCIAN CHURCH FATHER
THE THEOLOGICAL ORATIONS

The true Christ, the divine and heavenly Logos, the only High Priest of the world, the only King of all creation, the only Archprophet of prophets of the Father.

EUSEBIUS OF CAESAREA (C. 260-341)
THEOLOGIAN AND "FATHER OF CHURCH HISTORY"
ECCLESIASTICAL HISTORY

Jesus has been the subject of a hundred or so films, from Edison's *The Passion Play at Oberammergau* in 1898 to a quartet of Stan Brakhage experimental shorts in 2001. . . . The Messiah has been portrayed with stolid reverence (in Franco Zeffirelli's *Jesus of Nazareth*) and Surrealist blasphemy (Luis Bunuel's *L'Age d'Or*). Often he sings: in *Godspell* and *Jesus Christ Superstar*, in a born-again Bollywood musical and in the Canadian kung-fu horror comedy *Jesus Christ Vampire Hunter*.

"THE PASSION OF MEL GIBSON"
TIME MAGAZINE, 27 JANUARY 2003

God had an only son, and He was a missionary and a physician.

DAVID LIVINGSTONE (1813-1873)
SCOTTISH DOCTOR, MISSIONARY AND EXPLORER OF AFRICA

The vision of his glory ignites our hearts with
passionate anticipation, challenging us to live
faithfully every day, every hour, every moment in the
light of the imminent return of the One who
alone is worthy as . . .

The Alpha and the Omega
The Son of Man
The Son of God
The Great High Priest
The Light of the World
The Everlasting Father
The Commander of the Lord's Army
The Avenger of His People
The Lion of Judah
The Lamb Who was Slain
The Rider Called Faithful and True
The Word of God
The Final Judge
The Lord of Lords
and
The King of Kings.

ANNE GRAHAM LOTZ
BIBLE TEACHER AND FOUNDER OF ANGEL MINISTRIES
THE VISION OF HIS GLORY, 1996

Away in a manger, no crib for a bed,
The little Lord Jesus laid down His sweet head.
The stars in the sky looked down where he lay,
The little Lord Jesus asleep on the hay.

"AWAY IN A MANGER"
TRADITIONAL CHRISTMAS CAROL
(WORDS BY UNKNOWN AUTHOR;
MUSIC BY JAMES R. MURRAY, 1841-1905)

In his life, Christ is an example, showing us how to live; in his death, he is a sacrifice, satisfying for our sins; in his resurrection, a conqueror; in his ascension, a king; in his intercession, a high priest.

MARTIN LUTHER (1485-1546)
GERMAN MONK, THEOLOGIAN AND
LEADER OF THE PROTESTANT REFORMATION

O Lord Jesus Christ, Who art the Way, the Truth, and the Life, we pray Thee suffer us not to stray from Thee, who art the Way, nor to distrust Thee, who art the Truth, nor to rest in any other thing than Thee, who art the Life. Teach us by Thy Holy Spirit what to believe, what to do, and wherein to take our rest.

DESIDERIUS ROTTERDAMUS ERASMUS (C. 1469-1536)
DUTCH CHRISTIAN HUMANIST

And did those feet in ancient time
Walk upon England's mountains green?
And was the holy Lamb of God
On England's pleasant pastures seen?

And did the Countenance Divine
Shine forth upon our clouded hills?
And was Jerusalem builded here
Among these dark Satanic mills?

WILLIAM BLAKE (1757-1827)
BRITISH POET, ARTIST AND MYSTIC
"JERUSALEM"

Undergoing Jesus must be the center of any Christian
spirituality. . . . Jesus is the vine, the blood,
the pulse, and the heart.

RONALD ROLHEISER
CANADIAN CATHOLIC PRIEST AND SPIRITUAL WRITER
THE HOLY LONGING, 1999

God's Son becomes to all those who turn to him
their nurse, teacher, brother, counsellor, physician
and saviour, giving them strength, wisdom,
comfort, power and glory.

AUTHOR UNKNOWN (SECOND OR THIRD CENTURY)
EPISTLE TO DIOGNETUS

The cross for the first time revealed God in terms of weakness and lowliness and suffering; even, humanly speaking, of absurdity. He was seen thenceforth in the image of the most timid, most gentle, and most vulnerable of all living creatures—a lamb. Agnus Dei!

MALCOLM MUGGERIDGE (1903-1990)
BRITISH JOURNALIST AND MAGAZINE EDITOR
JESUS REDISCOVERED, 1969

Rest of the weary,
Joy of the sad,
Hope of the dreary,
Light of the glad,
Home of the stranger,
Strength to the end,
Refuge from danger,
Saviour and Friend!

JOHN SAMUEL BEWLEY MONSELL (1811-1875)
ENGLISH HYMN WRITER AND POET
HYMN, "REST OF THE WEARY," 1861

There is no harm in thinking that Christ is in bread. The harm is in the expectation of His presence in gunpowder.

JOHN RUSKIN (1819-1900)
ENGLISH ART AND SOCIAL CRITIC

Once I was able to cut through the fog still clinging from my own upbringing, my opinion of Jesus changed remarkably. Brilliant, untamed, tender, creative, merciful, clever, loving, irreducible, paradoxically humble—Jesus stands up to scrutiny. He is who I want my God to be.

PHILIP YANCEY
AMERICAN AWARD-WINNING WRITER
THE JESUS I NEVER KNEW, 1995

Consider all the titles Jesus could have used to define himself on earth: King of kings, the great I AM, the Beginning and the End, the Lord of All, Jehovah, High and Holy. All of these and a dozen others would have been appropriate. But Jesus didn't use them. Instead, he called himself the Son of Man.

MAX LUCADO
AMERICAN PASTOR AND AUTHOR
AND THE ANGELS WERE SILENT, 1992

Immanuel—God with us in our nature, in our sorrow, in our daily work, in our punishment, in our death, and now with us, or rather we with Him, in resurrection, ascension, triumph and Second Advent splendor.

CHARLES HADDON SPURGEON (1834–1892)
ENGLISH NONCONFORMIST PREACHER

I shall give you one word to express everything
which you have lost: and this word is "Jesus."
. . . Here by "Jesus" I mean all goodness, everlasting
wisdom, love and sweetness, your joy, your dignity
and your eternal happiness, your God, your Lord
and your salvation.

WALTER HILTON (FOURTEENTH CENTURY)
ENGLISH SPIRITUAL WRITER AND AUGUSTINIAN CANON
THE SCALE OF PERFECTION

No picture of the Christ more dear to us, than this of
the unlimited healing of whatever disease of body or
soul. In its blessed indefiniteness it conveys the
infinite potential of relief, whatever misery fall on
us, or whatever care or sorrow oppress us. He must
be blind, indeed, who sees not in this Physician the
Divine Healer; in this Christ the Light of the World.

ALFRED EDERSHEIM (1825-1889)
ANGLICAN BIBLICAL SCHOLAR

Christ is the desire of nations, the joy of angels, the
delight of the Father. What solace then must that
soul be filled with, that has the possession
of Him to all eternity!

JOHN BUNYAN (1628-1688)
ENGLISH WRITER AND NONCONFORMIST PREACHER

What are the key features of a good leader? . . . I pick out six themes of Jesus as visionary, servant leader, teacher, coach, radical and healer.

PETER SHAW
MIRRORING JESUS AS LEADER, 2004

Thou hast conquered, O pale Galilean.

ALGERNON CHARLES SWINBURNE (1837-1909)
ENGLISH POET AND CRITIC
"HYMN TO PROSPERINE"

There has never been a better raconteur than Jesus of Nazareth.

HARVEY COX
PROFESSOR OF DIVINITY AT HARVARD UNIVERSITY
THE SEDUCTION OF THE SPIRIT, 1973

It is the business of our human being to know Christ, and nothing else is our business. If it is true that we are made into the image of God, the sole, paramount, all-including and absorbing business of existence is to know that image of God in which we are made, to know it in the living Son of God— the one only ideal man.

GEORGE MACDONALD (1824-1905)
SCOTTISH NOVELIST, POET AND PASTOR
"DIVINE AND HUMAN RELATIONSHIP"

Jesus Christ makes Himself the touchstone.

OSWALD CHAMBERS (1874-1917)
SCOTTISH EVANGELIST AND WRITER
MY UTMOST FOR HIS HIGHEST, 1935

To be the way, the truth and the life; to be wisdom, righteousness, sanctification, resurrection; to be the whole world, the hope of the righteous, the heir of all things; to be that supreme head whereunto all power both in heaven and earth is given: these are not honours common unto Christ with other men; they are titles above the dignity and worth of any which were but a mere man.

RICHARD HOOKER (c. 1554-1600)
ENGLISH THEOLOGIAN

The name of Jesus is an ointment poured forth; It nourishes, and illumines, and stills the anguish of the soul.

ANGELUS SILESIUS (1624-1677)
GERMAN LUTHERAN POET

Our Lord Jesus Christ, my brethren, is our hero; a hero all the world wants.

GERARD MANLEY HOPKINS (1844-1889)
BRITISH POET AND JESUIT PRIEST
SERMON, 1879

Christ is the therapist for all humanity.

ROLLO MAY (1909-1994)
AMERICAN EXISTENTIALIST PSYCHOLOGIST

Do you think you're what they say you are?

TIM RICE AND ANDREW LLOYD-WEBBER
ROCK OPERA *JESUS CHRIST SUPERSTAR*
FIRST PERFORMED ON BROADWAY, 1971

The Holy Shroud . . . a relic now preserved at Turin, for which the claim is made that it is the actual "clean linen cloth" in which Joseph of Arimathea wrapped the body of Jesus Christ (Matthew 27:59). This relic, though blackened by age, bears the faint but distinct impress of a human form both back and front. The cloth is about 13½ feet long and 4¼ feet wide. If the marks we perceive were caused by a human body, it is clear that the body (supine) was laid lengthwise along one half of the shroud while the other half was doubled back over the head to cover the whole front of the body from the face to the feet.

THE CATHOLIC ENCYCLOPEDIA, 1907

Who is Christ? This is a question that has been
discussed for over nineteen centuries, and people
disclose something of their own character
by their reaction to it.

GEORGE APPLETON
MISSIONARY IN ASIA AND
ANGLICAN ARCHBISHOP IN JERUSALEM
JOURNEY FOR A SOUL, 1974

*B*ut what about you?" he asked. "Who do you say I am?"

MATTHEW 16:15

JESUS AND HISTORY

I am the Alpha and the Omega, the First and the Last, the Beginning and the End.

REVELATION 22:13

I know men; and I tell you that Jesus Christ is no mere man. Between him and every other person in the world there is no possible term of comparison. Caesar, Charlemagne and I have founded empires. But on what did we rest the creations of our genius? Upon force. Jesus Christ founded his empire upon love; and at this hour millions of men would die for him.

NAPOLEON BONAPARTE (1769–1821)
FRENCH GENERAL AND EMPEROR

Christianity introduced no new forms of government,
but a new spirit, which totally transformed
the old ones.

LORD ACTON (1834-1902)
BRITISH HISTORIAN

Man's ultimate destiny depends not on whether he
can learn new lessons or make new discoveries and
conquests, but on the acceptance of the lesson taught
him close upon two thousand years ago.

INSCRIPTION AT ENTRANCE TO
ROCKEFELLER CENTER, NEW YORK CITY

Who is the greatest leader in history? Of all the
names that might be given in response to that
question, one name stands out above the rest.
Jesus Christ.

BOB BRINER AND RAY PRITCHARD
THE LEADERSHIP LESSONS OF JESUS, 1998

The effects, then, of the work of Christ are even to
the unbeliever indisputable and historical. It expelled
cruelty; it curbed passion; it branded suicide; it
punished and repressed infanticide. There was hardly
a class whose wrongs it did not remedy. It rescued
the gladiator; it freed the slave; it protected the

captive; it nursed the sick; it sheltered the orphan; it elevated the woman; it shrouded as with a halo of sacred innocence the tender years of the child. In every region of life its ameliorating influence was felt. . . . It created the very conception of charity and broadened the limits of its obligation from the narrow circle of a neighbourhood to the widest horizons of the human race.

F. W. FARRAR (1831–1903)
CHAPLAIN TO THE QUEEN AND CANON OF WESTMINSTER
THE LIFE OF CHRIST, 1874

Time—the sequence of days, months and seasons—can be taken up into Christ, and so be sanctified and transfigured.

SEASONS OF THE SPIRIT, 1984
PREFACE TO READINGS SELECTED BY GEORGE EVERY,
RICHARD HARRIES AND KALLISTOS WARE

When the drama of history is over, Jesus Christ will stand alone on the stage. All the great figures of history . . . will realize that they have been but actors in a drama produced by another.

HELMUT THIELICKE (1908–1986)
GERMAN THEOLOGIAN

The first Christians were Jews. They differed from their fellow-countrymen by their faith that in Jesus of Nazareth the Messiah of the nation's expectation had now come. . . . If something new had happened, it was the action of one and the same God, Creator of the world, Lord of history, the God of Abraham, Isaac, Jacob, and the twelve patriarchs. His new word to his people must be consistent with that spoken in the past by the prophets.

HENRY CHADWICK
BRITISH THEOLOGIAN AND HEAD OF CHRIST CHURCH,
OXFORD, AND PETERHOUSE, CAMBRIDGE
THE EARLY CHURCH, 1993

As to Jesus of Nazareth, my opinion of whom you particularly desire, I think the system of morals and his religion, as he left them to us, the best the world ever saw or is likely to see; but I apprehend it has received numerous corrupting influences.

BENJAMIN FRANKLIN (1706–1790)
AMERICAN STATESMAN, INVENTOR AND SCIENTIST
LETTER TO THE PRESIDENT OF YALE COLLEGE, 1790

I have always considered Christ to be one of the greatest revolutionaries in the history of humanity.

FIDEL CASTRO
CUBAN PRESIDENT AND MARXIST REVOLUTIONARY

The achievement of Christ, in founding by His single will and power a structure so durable and universal, is like no other achievement which history accords. The masterpieces of the men of action are coarse and common in comparison with it, and the masterpieces of speculation flimsy and unsubstantial. When we speak of it, the common phrases of admiration fail us altogether.

SIR J. R. SEELEY (1834–1895)
BRITISH PROFESSOR OF LATIN AND HISTORY
*ECCE HOMO: A SURVEY OF THE LIFE
AND WORK OF JESUS CHRIST*, 1865

Imagine, for example, these responses from different observers, all of whom have heard and seen exactly the same words and deeds from that historical Jesus:

He's dangerous, let's oppose him.
He's criminal, let's execute him.
He's divine, let's follow him.

A historical account must be able to explain *all* of those different responses or it is inadequate to what happened.

JOHN DOMINIC CROSSAN
PROFESSOR OF BIBLICAL STUDIES
THE ESSENTIAL JESUS, 1998

The most potent figure, not only in the history of
religion, but in world history as a whole, is Jesus
Christ: the maker of one of the few revolutions
which have lasted. Millions of men and women for
century after century have found his life and teaching
overwhelmingly significant and moving. And there is
ample reason . . . why this should still be so.

MICHAEL GRANT
PRESIDENT OF THE CLASSICAL ASSOCIATION OF ENGLAND
JESUS, 1977

More books have been written, more songs have
been composed, and more lives have been given in
the name of Jesus Christ than of any other person
who ever lived. The beginning of his life on earth
was the beginning of our calendar, and the end of his
life on earth was the most dramatic event in history.
Even though Jesus left this world nearly two
thousand years ago, more than two billion people
living today identify with him in one way or another
by calling themselves Christians. By all
measurements, Jesus is the central
figure of the human race.

BRUCE BICKEL AND STAN JANTZ
WHY JESUS MATTERS, 2003

We do not need Christ to tell us that the world is full of trouble. But we do need his explanation of history if its troubles are not to be meaningless. In his life, death and resurrection, history comes to focus.

EUGENE H. PETERSON
AMERICAN PRESBYTERIAN CHURCH PASTOR AND WRITER
REVERSED THUNDER, 1988

The character of Jesus has not only been the highest pattern of virtue, but the strongest incentive in its practice, and has exerted so deep an influence, that it may be truly said that the simple record of three short years of active life has done more to regenerate and to soften mankind than all the disquisitions of philosophers and all the exhortations of moralists.

W. E. H. LECKY (WILLIAM EDWARD HARTPOLE LECKY)
(1838-1903)
IRISH HISTORIAN

Jesus was the greatest religious genius that ever lived. His beauty is eternal and his reign will never end. He is in every respect unique and nothing can be compared with him.

ERNEST RENAN (1823-1892)
FRENCH PHILOSOPHER AND THEOLOGIAN

He was born in an obscure village, the child of a peasant woman. He grew up in another village, where he worked in a carpenter shop until he was thirty. Then for three years he was an itinerant preacher.

He never wrote a book. He never held an office. He never traveled more than two hundred miles from the place where he was born. He did none of the things one usually associates with greatness.

He was only thirty-three when the tide of public opinion turned against him. He was turned over to his enemies and went through the mockery of a trial. He was nailed to a cross between two thieves. When he was dead, he was laid in a borrowed grave.

Nineteen centuries have come and gone, and today he is the central figure of the human race and leader of mankind's progress.

All the armies that ever marched, all the navies that ever sailed, all the kings that ever reigned, have not affected the life of man as much as that One Solitary Life.

AUTHOR UNKNOWN
"ONE SOLITARY LIFE," QUOTED IN CALVIN MILLER,
THE BOOK OF JESUS, 1996

The greatest man in history was the poorest.

RALPH WALDO EMERSON (1803–1882)
AMERICAN ESSAYIST, POET AND PHILOSOPHER

Revelation, in the Christian view, is not synonymous with social progress; it is not the actualizing of the immanent possibilities of history. Rather, in the person of Jesus God has broken into history in a way that transcends the possibilities of history as such.

PAUL K. JEWETT
PROFESSOR AT FULLER THEOLOGICAL SEMINARY
GOD, CREATION AND REVELATION, 1991

In his own lifetime Jesus made no impact on history. This is something that I cannot but regard as a special dispensation on God's part, and, I like to think, yet another example of the ironical humour which informs so many of his purposes. To me, it seems highly appropriate that the most important figure in all history should thus escape the notice of the memoirists, diarists, commentators, all the tribe of chroniclers who even then existed.

MALCOLM MUGGERIDGE (1903-1990)
BRITISH JOURNALIST AND MAGAZINE EDITOR

Christ is the most unique person in history. No man can write a history of the human race without giving first and foremost place to the penniless teacher of Nazareth.

H. G. WELLS (1866-1946)
ENGLISH NOVELIST AND POPULAR HISTORIAN

Our modern interest in the history of the human life
of Jesus has brought great and permanent gains to
our knowledge of Him, but there are definite limits
to the value of that knowledge for the Christian
faith. . . . The centre of gravity of the New Testament
is not on earth but in heaven.

H. WHEELER ROBINSON (1872–1945)
PRINCIPAL, REGENT'S PARK COLLEGE, OXFORD UNIVERSITY
THE CHRISTIAN EXPERIENCE OF THE HOLY SPIRIT, 1928

Those who would loosen the bolts that hold
Christianity to its massive implacement in history
would make it dependent on their own subjective
ideas. . . . The Gospels give the picture of a definite,
potent awe-inspiring personality. They carry
a conviction of reality.

LESLIE BADHAM
CHAPLAIN TO HER MAJESTY THE QUEEN
VERDICT ON JESUS, 1950

The sages and heroes of history are receding from us,
and history contracts the record of their deeds into a
narrower page. But time has no power over the
name and deeds and words of Jesus Christ.

WILLIAM ELLERY CHANNING (1780–1842)
AMERICAN UNITARIAN THEOLOGIAN AND PASTOR

The supreme miracle of Christ's character lies in this:
that He combines within Himself, as no other figure
in human history has ever done, the
qualities of every race.

C. F. ANDREWS (1871-1940)
(CHARLES FREER ANDREWS)
ENGLISH MISSIONARY IN INDIA
WHAT I OWE TO CHRIST, 1932

The belief in that truth which was revealed through
Christ—whether man is passionately opposed to it, or
whether he makes every effort to realize it as his
own destiny—has been *the* driving force of
history ever since.

ERICH FRANK (1883-1949)
GERMAN PHILOSOPHER
PHILOSOPHICAL UNDERSTANDING AND RELIGIOUS TRUTH, 1945

Jesus, or Joshua, which is the same name, means
"saviour." It is the Christian belief that one of the
many men in history who bore this name was
literally the Saviour of the World. And it is for this
reason that the Western World divides history itself
into the time before and after the birth of Jesus.

A. N. WILSON
ENGLISH JOURNALIST AND BIOGRAPHER
JESUS: A LIFE, 1992

I wish he would come in my lifetime so that I could take my crown and lay it at his feet.

QUEEN VICTORIA (1819–1901)
LONGEST-REIGNING BRITISH MONARCH

History, as it refers merely to human events, is a pleasing and interesting subject; but that which relates to our immortal interest certainly claims our most serious regard. The mind of man cannot be more delightfully employed than in the contemplation of the wisdom and goodness of the Great Creator of the Universe, who, by means the least thought of and imagined, confirmed and established that glorious Gospel, on which depend all the sinner's hopes of eternal salvation.

JOHN FLEETWOOD
ENGLISH CLERGYMAN
THE LIFE OF OUR LORD AND SAVIOUR JESUS CHRIST, 1826

The whole meaning of Christ cannot emerge from past history; indeed what it means for the risen Christ to be saviour in the world today will go on expanding until the end of time.

PAUL S. FIDDES
PRINCIPAL, REGENT'S PARK COLLEGE, OXFORD UNIVERSITY
PAST EVENT AND PRESENT SALVATION:
THE CHRISTIAN IDEA OF ATONEMENT, 1989

All the world would be Christian if they were taught
the pure Gospel of Christ!

THOMAS JEFFERSON (1743-1826)
U.S. PRESIDENT AND STATESMAN

The revelation made by Jesus Christ and the religion
He established were undeniably intended for all men,
in all places, and in all ages to the end of the world.

JEAN-NICOLAS GROU (1731-1803)
FRENCH JESUIT PRIEST
THE SCHOOL OF JESUS CHRIST, TRANS. 1932

[Jesus Christ] being the holiest among the mighty,
the mightiest among the holy, lifted with his pierced
hands empires off their hinges, and turned the
streams of centuries out of their channel, and
still governs the ages.

JEAN PAUL RICHTER (1863-1925)
GERMAN NOVELIST AND WRITER

The resurrection of Christ was what called the
Church into being, and turned a group of shattered,
demoralised men into evangelists who, against
all odds, gave a new direction to history.

F. RUSSELL BARRY (1890-1976)
ANGLICAN BISHOP OF SOUTHWELL

Every human being is able to become contemporary
only with the time in which he is living—and then
with one more, with Christ's life upon the earth, for
Christ's life upon the earth, the sacred history,
stands alone by itself, outside history.

SØREN KIERKEGAARD (1813–1855)
DANISH LUTHERAN PHILOSOPHER AND THEOLOGIAN
PRACTICE IN CHRISTIANITY, 1848

Jesus of Nazareth . . . is the point at which is
perceived the crimson thread which runs through all
history. *Christ*—the righteousness of God himself—
is the theme of this perception.

KARL BARTH (1886–1968)
SWISS REFORMED THEOLOGIAN
"ON THE EPISTLE TO THE ROMANS," 1921

I believe that he belongs not only to Christianity but
to the entire world, to all races and people; it matters
little under what flag, name, or doctrine they may
work, profess a faith, or worship a God
inherited from the ancestors.

MAHATMA GANDHI (MOHANDAS KARAMCHAND GANDHI)
(1869–1948)
INDIAN STATESMAN AND PACIFIST

I find the name of Jesus Christ written on the top
of every page of modern history.

GEORGE BANCROFT (1800–1891)
AMERICAN HISTORIAN AND DIPLOMAT

Christ is the great central fact in the world's history.
To him everything looks forward or backward. All
the lines of history converge upon him. All the great
purposes of God culminate in him. The greatest and
most momentous fact which the history of the
world records is the fact of his birth.

CHARLES HADDON SPURGEON (1834–1892)
ENGLISH NONCONFORMIST PREACHER

Jesus Christ belonged to the true race of the
prophets. He saw with an open eye the mystery of
the soul. Drawn by its severe harmony, ravished with
its beauty, he lived in it, and had his being there.
Alone in all history he estimated the
greatness of man.

RALPH WALDO EMERSON (1803–1882)
AMERICAN ESSAYIST, POET AND PHILOSOPHER
HARVARD DIVINITY SCHOOL ADDRESS, 1838

Nothing is more abhorrent to the tyrant than
the service of Christ.

GIROLAMO SAVONAROLA (1452–1498)
ITALIAN DOMINICAN PREACHER

Christians think of the cross and passion of Christ as
the great turning-point of history, and this is
justified because in Christ there was this decisive
turning to the Father. There had emerged a new
righteousness that had proved stronger than sin.

JOHN MACQUARRIE
SCOTTISH THEOLOGIAN
PRINCIPLES OF CHRISTIAN THEOLOGY, 1977

The Jesus Christ of the New Testament is in our
actual history, in history as we remember and live it,
as it shapes our present faith and action. And this
Jesus Christ is a definite person, one and the same
whether he appears as a man of flesh and blood
or as risen Lord.

H. RICHARD NIEBUHR (1894–1962)
PROFESSOR OF CHRISTIAN ETHICS AT YALE DIVINITY SCHOOL
CHRIST AND CULTURE, 1951

Jesus means something to our world because a mighty spiritual force streams forth from him and flows through our being also. This fact can neither be shaken nor confirmed by any historical discovery. It is the solid foundation of Christianity.

ALBERT SCHWEITZER (1875–1965)
ALSACE-BORN MUSICIAN, NEW TESTAMENT SCHOLAR,
MEDICAL MISSIONARY AND NOBEL PEACE PRIZE WINNER

Jesus Christ is the same yesterday and today and forever.

HEBREWS 13:8

SPIRITUAL LEGACY

I am the resurrection and the life. He who believes in me will live, even though he dies; and whoever lives and believes in me will never die.

JOHN 11:25-26

The Christian ideal has not been tried and found wanting. It has been found difficult; and left untried.

G. K. CHESTERTON (1874-1936)
(GILBERT KEITH CHESTERTON)
ENGLISH ESSAYIST, NOVELIST AND POET
"WHAT'S WRONG WITH THE WORLD"

It is a bad world, Donatus, an incredibly bad world. But I have discovered in the midst of it a quiet and holy people who have learned a great secret. They have found a joy which is a thousand times better than any pleasure of our sinful life. They are despised and persecuted, but they care not. They are masters of their souls. They have overcome the world. These

people, Donatus, are the Christians—and
I am one of them.

ST. CYPRIAN (C. 200-258)
BISHOP OF CARTHAGE AND MARTYR

The Bible tells us that we are "the body of Christ."
This description of the community of faith is not
some romantic metaphor but is a genuine reality.
Jesus Christ through the Spirit continues to live
within his Church, and our sufferings are his
sufferings. . . . And these sufferings are redemptive;
they are actually used of God to change and
transform and draw people into the way of Christ.

RICHARD J. FOSTER
QUAKER THEOLOGIAN, WRITER AND
PROFESSOR OF SPIRITUAL FORMATION
PRAYER: FINDING THE HEART'S TRUE HOME, 1992

The point is that Jesus, while on earth, was human,
and that he gave us a revelation of the maximum
effect that one human being has ever been able to
exercise upon others. . . . This demonstration . . . was
and permanently remains the most heartening thing
which has ever happened to the human race.

MICHAEL GRANT
PRESIDENT OF THE CLASSICAL ASSOCIATION OF ENGLAND
JESUS, 1977

I am part of the organism through which Christ
continues to live in the world. I too am required to
incarnate something of his all-generous and
redeeming spirit, share my knowledge of Him, give
myself without stint to heal and save other children
of God at my own cost. How does
my life stand *that* test?

EVELYN UNDERHILL (1875-1941)
ENGLISH SPIRITUAL WRITER
LIGHT OF CHRIST, 1944

Perhaps after reading expert after expert, listening to
argument after argument, seeing the answers to
question after question, and testing the evidence
with your logic and common sense, you've found, as I
have, that the case for Christ is conclusive.

LEE STROBEL
AMERICAN JOURNALIST
THE CASE FOR CHRIST, 1998

What are we to make of Jesus Christ? This is a
question which has, in a sense, a frantically comic
side. For the real question is not what are we to
make of Christ, but what is He to make of us?

C. S. LEWIS (CLIVE STAPLES LEWIS) (1898-1963)
IRISH LITERARY SCHOLAR,
CHRISTIAN APOLOGIST AND WRITER
QUOTED IN *THE JOYFUL CHRISTIAN,* 1996

There was an extremeness in the hopefulness of Jesus that sets him apart from all other men who expect lesser glories or more frequently, no glory at all. Average morality presupposes complacency tempered by a little cynicism, or resignation qualified by moderate expectations of good. Intense anticipation of supernal good must result in a transformation of ethics.

H. RICHARD NIEBUHR (1894–1962)
PROFESSOR OF CHRISTIAN ETHICS AT YALE DIVINITY SCHOOL
CHRIST AND CULTURE, 1951

To live as Christians, to feel as Christians, to think as Christians in a society which is not Christian, when we see, hear, and read almost nothing which does not offend or contradict Christianity . . . we are continually tempted to diminish or adapt our truth, in order to lessen the distance which separates our ways of thinking from those of the world, or indeed, and sometimes in all sincerity, in the hope of rendering Christianity more acceptable to the world and of seconding its work of salvation.

ÉTIENNE HENRY GILSON (1884–1978)
FRENCH PROFESSOR OF MEDIEVAL PHILOSOPHY
CHRISTIANITY AND PHILOSOPHY, 1939

There are times when we can never meet the future with sufficient elasticity of mind, especially if we are locked in the contemporary systems of thought. We can do worse than remember a principle which both gives us a firm Rock and leaves us the maximum elasticity for our minds: the principle: Hold to Christ, and for the rest be totally uncommitted.

HERBERT BUTTERFIELD (1900–1979)
BRITISH HISTORIAN AND PHILOSOPHER

If the essence of Christianity is neither a creed, nor a code, nor a cult, what is it? It is Christ! It is not primarily a system of any kind; it is a person, and a personal relationship to that person.

JOHN R. W. STOTT
RECTOR EMERITUS OF ALL SOULS CHURCH, LONDON
CHRISTIAN BASICS, 1991

Christ is the Word who shouted all things into being and who continually calls each of us into fuller being, every day, every minute, right now.

MADELEINE L'ENGLE
AMERICAN AWARD-WINNING WRITER

Heaven and hell are not places far away, but near us. Everything depends on what we do with Jesus.

ERWIN LUTZER
CANADIAN PASTOR OF THE MOODY CHURCH
CRIES FROM THE CROSS, 2002

When Christ came into the world, peace was sung;
and when He went out of the world,
peace was bequeathed.

SIR FRANCIS BACON (1561-1626)
ENGLISH LAWYER, PHILOSOPHER AND ESSAYIST

The centre of God's salvific design is Jesus Christ,
who by his death and resurrection transforms the
universe and makes it possible for each man to reach
fulfilment as a human being. This fulfilment
embraces every aspect of humanity; body and spirit,
individual and society, person and cosmos,
time and eternity.

FIRST CONFERENCE OF LATIN AMERICAN BISHOPS
AT MEDELLIN, 1969

Despite the controversy—or profiting from it—
Passion is expected to be a box office boon of
biblical proportions, putting Gibson's version of
the greatest story ever told in a league with
the greatest story ever sold.

CBS EVENING NEWS, FEBRUARY 18, 2004
(REPORTING ON THE RELEASE OF THE FILM,
THE PASSION OF THE CHRIST)

No other religion or philosophy promises glorified
bodies, hearts and minds. Only in the Gospel of
Jesus Christ do hurting people find
such incredible hope.

JONI EARECKSON TADA
FOUNDER OF JONI AND FRIENDS MINISTRIES

How many observe Christ's birthday! How few his
precepts! O! 'tis easier to keep holidays
than commandments.

BENJAMIN FRANKLIN (1706-1790)
AMERICAN STATESMAN, INVENTOR AND SCIENTIST

Christ is the centre of all, and the goal to
which all tends.

BLAISE PASCAL (1623-1662)
FRENCH PHILOSOPHER, MATHEMATICIAN AND PHYSICIST

If Jesus Christ were to come today, people would not
even crucify him. They would ask him to dinner, and
hear what he had to say, and make fun of it.

THOMAS CARLYLE (1795-1881)
SCOTTISH HISTORIAN AND POLITICAL PHILOSOPHER
QUOTED IN D. A. WILSON, *CARLYLE AT HIS ZENITH*, 1927

The distinction between Christians and other people lies not in country or language or customs. Christians do not dwell in special houses or districts of cities, nor do they use a peculiar dialect, nor do they have any extraordinary customs. Their teaching has not been discovered by the intellect or thought of clever men, nor do they advocate any human doctrine. Wherever they live they follow the local customs, eating the food that local people eat, living in ordinary houses, and wearing clothes indistinguishable from those of their neighbors. It is in their attitudes that they are distinctive. They live in the lands where they were born, but see themselves not as owners of that land, but as sojourners; they are strangers on this earth. To them, every foreign land is like their fatherland, and every fatherland like a foreign land. They behave as perfect and upright citizens, according to the law of the state they inhabit; but they see themselves as citizens of another state, the kingdom of God.

AUTHOR UNKNOWN (SECOND OR THIRD CENTURY)
"EPISTLE TO DIOGNETUS"

Even as you read these words, someone in the world
is deciding that Jesus Christ is still alive. Although
the membership of the Christian Churches would
seem to be in irreversible decline, there remains no
shortage of persons from all over the globe who
would wish to attest to the living presence
of Jesus in their lives.

A. N. WILSON
ENGLISH JOURNALIST AND BIOGRAPHER
JESUS: A LIFE, 1992

Christ beats the drum, but he does not press men;
Christ is served with voluntaries.

JOHN DONNE (1572–1631)
ENGLISH POET AND DIVINE
SERMONS, NO. 39

The world may argue against Christianity as an
institution, but there is no convincing argument
against a person who through the Spirit of God
has been made Christlike.

BILLY GRAHAM (WILLIAM FRANKLIN GRAHAM JR.)
AMERICAN EVANGELICAL LEADER AND WRITER
THE SECRET OF HAPPINESS, 1955

Of all the systems of morality, ancient or modern,
which have come under my observation, none
appears to me so pure as that of Jesus.

THOMAS JEFFERSON (1743–1826)
U.S. PRESIDENT AND STATESMAN

I have read the stories of Jesus many times, but I
have never lost that sense of new discovery and
excitement. Jesus remains as compelling as ever.

JOHN DRANE
BRITISH SPIRITUAL TEACHER AND WRITER

Was not Jesus an extremist for love? . . . So the
question is not whether we will be extremists,
but what kind of extremists we will be.

MARTIN LUTHER KING JR. (1929–1968)
AMERICAN CIVIL RIGHTS LEADER

None of us has lived up to the teaching of Christ.

ELEANOR ROOSEVELT (1884–1962)
AMERICAN HUMANITARIAN AND DIPLOMAT

I have never been able to reconcile myself to the
gaieties of the Christmas season. They have appeared
to me to be so inconsistent with the life
and teaching of Jesus.

How I wish America could lead the way by devoting the season to a real moral stocktaking and emphasizing consecration to the service of mankind for which Jesus lived and died on the Cross.

MAHATMA GANDHI (MOHANDAS KARAMCHAND GANDHI)
(1869–1948)
INDIAN STATESMAN AND PACIFIST
WHAT JESUS MEANS TO ME, 1959
(ORIGINALLY FROM A 1931 CHRISTMAS-DAY TALK)

The great part of Christianity is wholeheartedly to want to become a Christian.

DESIDERIUS ROTTERDAMUS ERASMUS (1467–1536)
DUTCH HUMANIST SCHOLAR

If the world is ever conquered for Christ, it will be by every one doing their own work, filling their own sphere, holding their own post, and saying to Jesus, Lord, what wilt thou have me do.

THOMAS GUTHRIE (1803–1873)
SCOTTISH DIVINE AND SOCIAL REFORMER

When has so sudden and so bright a light of faith been kindled in the world, as by the preaching of the Name of Jesus?

ST. BERNARD OF CLAIRVAUX (1091–1153)
FRENCH MONK AND FOUNDER OF THE CISTERCIAN ORDER
SERMON ON THE SONG OF SONGS

The most excellent study for expanding the soul, is the science of Christ, and Him crucified, and the knowledge of the Godhead in the glorious Trinity. Nothing will so enlarge the intellect, nothing so magnify the whole soul of a man, as a devout, earnest, continued investigation of the great subject of the Deity.

JAMES I. PACKER
BRITISH EVANGELICAL THEOLOGIAN AND WRITER
KNOWING GOD, 1973

It does not take a perfect church to introduce a man to the perfect Christ.

RICHARD WOODSOME
CHRISTIAN WRITER

The Lord who has vacated his tomb has not vacated his throne.

GEORGE R. BEASLEY-MURRAY (1916–2000)
BRITISH BAPTIST BIBLE SCHOLAR

The sincere Christian is progressive—never at his journey's end till he gets to heaven. This keeps him always in motion, advancing in his desires and endeavours forward.

WILLIAM GURNALL (1616–1679)
ENGLISH PURITAN CLERGYMAN

This is not an age in which to be a soft Christian.

FRANCIS A. SCHAEFFER (1912–1984)
AMERICAN PRESBYTERIAN MINISTER AND SPEAKER

The glory of Christianity is to conquer
by forgiveness.

WILLIAM BLAKE (1757–1827)
BRITISH POET, ARTIST AND MYSTIC

Some say that ever 'gainst that season comes
Wherein our Saviour's birth is celebrated,
The bird of dawning singeth all night long;
And then, they say, no spirit dare stir abroad;
The nights are wholesome; then no planets strike,
No fairy takes, nor witch hath power to charm,
So hallow'd and so gracious is the time.

WILLIAM SHAKESPEARE (1564–1616)
ENGLISH DRAMATIST
PLAY, *HAMLET*

The ascension of Christ is his liberation from all
restrictions of time and space. It does not represent
his removal from the earth, but his constant
presence everywhere on earth.

WILLIAM TEMPLE (1881–1944)
ANGLICAN ARCHBISHOP OF CANTERBURY AND WRITER

Christianity is the highest perfection of humanity.

SAMUEL JOHNSON (1709-1784)
ENGLISH POET AND CRITIC

No generation can claim to have plumbed to the depths the unfathomable riches of Christ. The Holy Spirit has promised to lead us step by step into the fullness of truth.

LEON JOSEPH SUENENS (1905-1996)
BELGIAN CARDINAL

Christianity, if false, is of no importance, and if true, of infinite importance. The one thing it cannot be is moderately important.

C. S. LEWIS (CLIVE STAPLES LEWIS) (1898-1963)
IRISH LITERARY SCHOLAR,
CHRISTIAN APOLOGIST AND WRITER

Where people are sincerely devoted to and follow Christ and dwell under the influence of his Holy Spirit, their stability and firmness through a divine blessing is at times like dew on the tender plants around them, and the weightiness of their spirit secretly works on the minds of others.

JOHN WOOLMAN (1720-1772)
AMERICAN QUAKER PREACHER

To restore all things in Christ.
(*Instaurare omnia in Christo.*)

MOTTO OF POPE PIUS X (1835-1914)

In Jesus we have met the one who has the authority
and power to forgive our fevered search to gain
security through deception, coercion, and
violence. . . . Thus in contrast to all societies built on
shared resentments and fears, Christian community is
formed by a story that enables its members to trust
the otherness of the other as the very sign of the
forgiving character of God's kingdom.

STANLEY HAUERWAS
AMERICAN PROFESSOR OF THEOLOGICAL ETHICS
*A COMMUNITY OF CHARACTER: TOWARD A CONSTRUCTIVE
CHRISTIAN SOCIAL ETHIC,* 1981

Christ was the word that spake it;
He took the bread and break it;
And what that word did make it,
That I believe and take it.

ELIZABETH I (1533-1603)
QUEEN OF ENGLAND FROM 1558

It is either Christ or chaos.

DAVID LLOYD GEORGE (1863-1945)
BRITISH PRIME MINISTER AND STATESMAN

Jesus' enduring relevance is based on his historically proven ability to speak to, to heal and empower the individual human condition.

DALLAS WILLARD
SOUTHERN BAPTIST MINISTER, THEOLOGIAN AND SCHOLAR

The Christian is not the one who had gone all the way with Christ. None of us has. The Christian is one who has found the right road.

CHARLES L. ALLEN
AMERICAN METHODIST PASTOR
WHEN THE HEART IS HUNGRY, 1955

I now most solemnly impress upon you the truth and beauty of the Christian Religion, as it came from Christ Himself, and the impossibility of your going far wrong if you humbly but heartily respect it.

CHARLES DICKENS (1812-1870)
ENGLISH NOVELIST
(LETTER TO HIS SON DEPARTING FOR AUSTRALIA)

Let's quit fiddling with religion and do something to bring the world to Christ.

BILLY SUNDAY (WILLIAM A. SUNDAY) (1862-1935)
AMERICAN EVANGELIST

Today, we think of Christ's power entering our lives in various ways—through the sense of forgiveness and love for God or through the awareness of truth, through special experiences or the infusion of the Spirit, through the presence of Christ in the inner life or through the power of ritual and liturgy or the preaching of the Word, through the communion of the saints or through a heightened consciousness of the depths and mystery of life. All of these are doubtlessly real and of some good effect. However, neither individually nor collectively do any of these ways reliably produce large numbers of people who really are like Christ and his closest followers throughout history. . . . What we need is a deeper insight into our practical relationship with God in redemption. . . . In other words, we must develop a psychologically sound theology of the spiritual life and of its disciplines to guide us.

DALLAS WILLARD
SOUTHERN BAPTIST MINISTER, THEOLOGIAN AND SCHOLAR
THE SPIRIT OF THE DISCIPLINES, 1988

The one mark of a saint is the moral originality which springs from abandonment to Jesus Christ.

OSWALD CHAMBERS (1874–1917)
SCOTTISH EVANGELIST AND WRITER
MY UTMOST FOR HIS HIGHEST, 1935

The Spirit of Christ is the spirit of missions, and the nearer we get to Him the more intensely missionary we must become.

HENRY MARTYN (1781–1812)
ANGLICAN MISSIONARY AND TRANSLATOR

Christ has given us the most glorious interpretation of life's meaning that man has ever had. The fatherhood of God, the fellowship of the Spirit, the sovereignty of righteousness, the law of love, the glory of service, the coming of the Kingdom, the eternal hope—there never was an interpretation of life to compare with that.

HARRY EMERSON FOSDICK (1878–1969)
AMERICAN LIBERAL BAPTIST MINISTER

The Church exists on earth [as] the means whereby Christ becomes active and carries out his purpose in the world; that is what it is for, and that is what makes it the Church, the life of his Spirit within it, rising out of its faith in him.

WILLIAM TEMPLE (1881–1944)
ANGLICAN ARCHBISHOP OF CANTERBURY AND WRITER

If a man cannot be a Christian in the place where he is, he cannot be a Christian anywhere.

HENRY WARD BEECHER (1813–1887)
AMERICAN CLERGYMAN AND ABOLITIONIST
LIFE THOUGHTS, 1858

Promoting self under the guise of promoting Christ is currently so common as to excite little notice.

A. W. TOZER (AIDEN WILSON TOZER) (1897–1963)
AMERICAN PASTOR AND WRITER
THE PURSUIT OF GOD, 1948

Christianity is not a matter of persuading people of particular ideas, but of inviting them to share in the greatness of Christ.

ST. IGNATIUS OF ANTIOCH (C. SECOND CENTURY)
BISHOP OF ANTIOCH IN SYRIA
"ON THE EPISTLE TO THE ROMANS"

I will come again, and receive you unto myself; that where I am, there ye may be also.

JOHN 14:3 (KJV)

GUIDE TO THEMES

The following indicative themes provide a guide for identifying quotations within each section.

JESUS AS GOD AND MAN
   Divinity, Eternity, Father, Flesh, Heaven, Humanity, Incarnation, Mediator, Mystery, Perfection, Revelation, Son of God, Trinity, Two Natures, Word

THE LIFE AND TEACHINGS OF JESUS
   Ethics, Gospel, Healing, Humility, Justice, Kingdom of God, Love, Miracles, Nativity, Peace, Prayer, Service, Truth, Wisdom

THE LOVE OF CHRIST
   Discipleship, Grace, Heart, Hope, Joy, Longing, Personal Relationship, Presence, Security, Vocation

LIFE IN CHRIST
   Belief, Commitment, Consecration, Example, Faith, Fellowship, Follow, Guidance, New Creation, Providence, Surrender, The Way, Witness

JESUS AS SAVIOR
   Atonement, Conversion, Deliverance, Lamb of God, Mercy, Redemption, Resurrection, Salvation, Sin

THE POWER OF THE CROSS
Burden, Crucifixion, Death, Denial, Paradox, Sorrow, Suffering, Symbol, Transformation, Tree, Triumph

IMAGES OF JESUS
Carpenter, Child, Counselor, Door, Friend, Healer, Holiness, Immanuel, Lamp, Leader, Logos, Lord, Names, Preacher, Priest, Shepherd, Teacher, Visions

JESUS AND HISTORY
Alpha and Omega, Charity, Empires, Government, Influence, Memory, Prophet, Revolution, Turning Point, Uniqueness, World

SPIRITUAL LEGACY
Body of Christ, Christianity, Christmas, Church, Community, Culture, Discipleship, Eternal Life, Glory, Goal, Holy Spirit, Hope, Mission, Morality, Peace, Relationship, Second Coming, Truth, Worship

SELECTED
BIBLIOGRAPHY

*M*any quotations in this collection already reference full authorship, source title, and/or date of publication. In addition, the author wishes to acknowledge the following secondary sources.

12,000 Inspirational Quotations: A Treasury of Spiritual Insights and Practical Wisdom, edited by Frank S. Mead. Springfield, Mass.: Federal Street Press, 2000 (originally published 1965).

12,000 Religious Quotations, edited by Frank S. Mead. Grand Rapids: Baker, 1989.

Barnes & Noble Book of Quotations, edited by Robert I. Fitzhenry. New York: Harper & Row, 1987.

Bartlett's Familiar Quotations, edited by Emily Morrison Beck. Boston: Little, Brown and Company, 15th ed., 1980.

Biblical Quotations: A Reference Guide, edited by Martin H. Manser. New York: Facts on File, Inc., 2001.

The Book of Catholic Quotations, edited by John Chapin. New York: Farrar, Straus and Cudahy, 1956.

The Book of Jesus, edited by Calvin Miller. New York: Simon & Schuster, 1996.

The Book of Positive Quotations, compiled by John Cook. Minneapolis: Fairview Press, 1993.

The Christian Quote Book, compiled by Rachel Quillin. Uhrichsville, Ohio: Barbour, 2004.

The Christian Theology Reader, edited by Alister E. McGrath. Oxford: Blackwell, 2nd ed., 2001.

Christianity: Two Thousand Years, edited by Richard Harries and Henry Mayr-Harting. Oxford: Oxford University Press, 2001.

Christology of the Later Fathers, edited by Edward Rochie Hardy. (The Library of Christian Classics, Vol. III). Philadelphia: Westminster Press, 1965.

The Columbia World of Quotations, edited by Robert Andrews, Mary Biggs and Michael Seidel. New York: Columbia University Press, 1996.

Concise Dictionary of Religious Quotations, compiled by William Neil. Oxford: Mowbrays, 1975.

Devotional Classics, edited by Richard J. Foster and James Bryan Smith. San Francisco: HarperSanFrancisco, 1993.

Disciplines for the Inner Life, Bob Benson Sr. and Michael W. Benson. Nashville: Thomas Nelson, 1989.

The Doubleday Christian Quotation Collection, compiled by Hannah Ward and Jennifer Wild. New York: Doubleday, 1998. (Originally published in England as *The Lion Christian Quotation Collection,* 1997).

The Doubleday Prayer Collection, selected by Mary Batchelor. New York: Doubleday, 1997. (Originally published in England as *The Lion Prayer Collection,* 1992).

Encarta Book of Quotations, edited by Bill Swainson. New York: St. Martin's Press, 2000.

An Encyclopedia of Compelling Quotations, compiled by R. Daniel Watkins. Peabody, Mass.: Hendrickson Publishers, 2001.

Glimpses of the Divine, Bishop Cyril Bulley. Worthing, Sussex: Churchman Publishing Ltd., 1987.

God's Message for Each Day, Eugene H. Peterson. Nashville: J. Countryman/Thomas Nelson, 2004.

God's Word for Women. Uhrichsville, Ohio: Barbour, 2000.

The Great Thoughts, compiled by George Seldes. New York: Ballantine, 1985.

A Handbook of Christian Mysticism, Michael Cox. London: Crucible/Thorsons Publishing Group, 1986.

A Heritage of Great Evangelical Teaching. Nashville: Thomas Nelson, 1996.

His Miracles: The Most Moving Words Ever Written About the Miracles of Jesus. Brentwood, Tenn.: Integrity, 2004.

His Passion: Christ's Journey to the Resurrection. Brentwood, Tenn.: Integrity, 2004.

Hoyt's New Cyclopedia of Practical Quotations, compiled by Kate Louise Roberts. New York: Funk & Wagnalls, 1927.

The Hymnal for Worship and Celebration. Waco, Tex.: Word Music, 1986.

Inspiration: 2000 Years of Christian Wisdom. Oxford: Lion Publishing, 1999.

The International Thesaurus of Quotations, compiled by Rhoda Thomas Tripp. New York: Thomas Y. Crowell Company, 1970.

An Introduction to the Christian Faith, edited by Robin Keeley. Oxford: Lynx/Lion Publishing, 1982.

The Jesus Book, compiled by Michael F. McCauley. Chicago: The Thomas Moore Press, 1978.

Journey for a Soul, George Appleton. Glasgow: Collins Publishers, 1974.

The Knowing Jesus Study Bible, edited by Edward Hindson and Edward Dobson. Grand Rapids: Zondervan Publishing House, 1999.

Morrow's International Dictionary of Contemporary Quotations, compiled by Jonathon Green. New York: William Morrow and Company, 1982.

The New Encyclopedia of Christian Quotations, compiled by Mark Water. Alresford, Hampshire: John Hunt Publishing Ltd., 2000.

The New International Dictionary of Quotations, selected by Margaret Miner and Hugh Rawson. Harmondsworth: Penguin, 3rd ed., 2000.

The New Oxford Book of Christian Verse, edited by Donald Davie. Oxford: Oxford University Press, 1981.

The Oxford Book of Prayer, edited by George Appleton. Oxford: Oxford University Press, 1985.

The Oxford Dictionary of Quotations, edited by Elizabeth Knowles. Oxford:

Oxford University Press, 5th ed., 1999.

Oxford Readers: Jesus, edited by David F. Ford and Mike Higton. Oxford: Oxford University Press, 2002.

Quotations of Courage and Vision, compiled by Carl Hermann Voss. New York: Association Press, 1972.

Religious & Spiritual Quotations, edited by Geoffrey Parrinder. London: Routledge, 1990.

Roots of Faith, edited by Robert Van De Weyer. Grand Rapids: Eerdmans, 1997.

Simpson's Contemporary Quotations, compiled by James B. Simpson. Boston: Houghton Mifflin, 1988.

A Time to Pray, compiled by Philip Law. Nashville: Dimensions for Living, 1998.

Topical Encyclopedia of Living Quotations, edited by Sherwood Eliot Wirt and Kersten Beckstrom. Minneapolis: Bethany House, 1982.

The Treasures of Charles Spurgeon, compiled by Dan Harmon. Uhrichsville, Ohio: Barbour, 2004.

A Treasury of Biblical Quotations, edited by Anthony J. Castagno. Nashville: Thomas Nelson, 1980.

The Treasury of Christian Spiritual Classics. Nashville: Thomas Nelson, 1994.

Wade Cook's Power Quotes, compiled by Wade B. Cook. Seattle: Lighthouse Publishing Group, 1998.

The Westminster Collection of Christian Quotations, compiled by Martin H. Manser. Louisville: Westminster John Knox Press, 2001.

Wisdom for Christian Living, Matthew Henry. Uhrichsville, Ohio: Barbour, 2003.

A Woman's Treasury of Faith. Grand Rapids: Family Christian Press, 2004.

A Woman's Treasury of Hope. Grand Rapids: Family Christian Press, 2004.

The World Treasury of Modern Religious Thought, edited by Jaroslav Pelikan. Boston: Little, Brown and Company, 1990.

INDEX OF SOURCES

Each source lists one or more page numbers to locate quotations.

*From *The New International Version,* unless otherwise identified

HYMNS, SONGS AND POEMS *(BY TITLE)*

DEAR READERS,

Do you have a favorite quotation about Jesus? We at Bethany House Publishers would be privileged to consider your contributions for another collection of inspiring thoughts. Please send the full quotation, author, date, and other reference information to:

Dr. Isabella D. Bunn
℅ Bethany House Publishers
Editorial Department
11400 Hampshire Avenue South
Bloomington, Minnesota 55438

Or send an e-mail to: *editorial@bethanyhouse.com*

With thanks and best regards,
Isabella

Some of History's Most Powerful Thoughts

"The Gospel is not merely a book—it is a living power—a book surpassing all others. I never omit to read it, and every day with the same pleasure...."

—NAPOLEON BONAPARTE

Ancient scrolls and yesterday's newspapers alike have had something to say about the Bible. Isabella Bunn has compiled a remarkable collection of reactions to the Word of God in her book *444 Surprising Quotes About the Bible*.

444 Surprising Quotes About the Bible
Compiled by Isabella D. Bunn

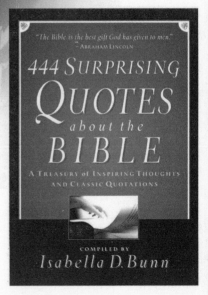

"The Bible is the best gift God has given to men."
~ ABRAHAM LINCOLN

444 SURPRISING
QUOTES
about the
BIBLE
A TREASURY of INSPIRING THOUGHTS
AND CLASSIC QUOTATIONS

COMPILED BY
Isabella D. Bunn

◆BETHANYHOUSE